WAIT! I Need to Overthink!
From Panicked and Trapped to Observant and Intentional

by Nick Trenton

www.NickTrenton.com

Table of Contents

CHAPTER 1: OWN WHAT YOU FEEL — 5

EMOTIONS: DATA, NOT DIRECTIVES — 6
THREE TYPES OF RUMINATION—AND HOW TO STOP — 19
ADJUST YOUR ASSUMPTIONS — 30

CHAPTER 2: FIND CLARITY — 43

UNLOAD WITH FREEWRITING — 44
ORGANIZE YOUR OVERWHELMED MIND WITH ANXIETY MAPPING — 50
TURN OFF THOSE FALSE ALARMS — 61

CHAPTER 3: GET GROUNDED — 73

DON'T TAKE YOUR OWN WORD FOR IT — 73
CHECK THE FACTS — 82
AVOID STRESS BY AVOIDING OVERCOMMITMENT — 91

CHAPTER 4: GATHER YOURSELF — 103

THE OBSERVING MIND: WATCH THOUGHTS . . . AND LET THEM GO — 104
GIVE YOUR ATTENTION A WORKOUT — 112
THE WORST CASE, THE BEST CASE, AND THE MOST LIKELY CASE — 120

CHAPTER 5: BE STILL — 131

WABI-SABI: MINDFUL IMPERFECTIONISM	132
LEARNING TO TOLERATE UNCERTAINTY	141
HOW TO CULTIVATE HELPFUL THINKING	156

CHAPTER 6: MOVE FORWARD — 171

OVERCHOICE: HOW TO AVOID ANALYSIS PARALYSIS	172
REVERSING THE ANXIETY SPIRAL	184
TRANSFORM OVERTHINKING INTO PROBLEM-SOLVING	193

Chapter 1: Own What You Feel

Most of us feel anxious about things now and again, and it's not unusual to get carried away with overthinking when it comes to big life decisions or challenging situations. But if you've picked up this book, there's a strong chance that your anxiety goes way beyond this. Chronic and habitual overthinking can damage relationships, interfere with work, and utterly exhaust you in the process.

The good news is that this is not something you're doomed to live with forever! Overthinking is a learned behavior, and that means it can be unlearned. In the chapters that follow, we'll be cutting through the angst and chaos and finding the clarity, courage, and compassion needed to live life without undue worry and stress.

Whether you struggle with self-regulation now and again or are dealing with more entrenched thought patterns, the simple and effective approaches covered in this book will help you take back control. When your mind is racing at a million miles an hour, it can be hard to know what to do with yourself or where to start. Fortunately for us, the first step is the easiest: All that's required is for us to become aware.

What are you feeling?

Emotions: Data, Not Directives

Our first task is to understand our experience, name it, and learn to understand exactly how it functions. You may think, "I feel anxious!" but what does that word actually mean? If you're an anxious overthinker, anxiety may feel like a messy mix of all the following:

- Overwhelmed
- On edge
- Irritated and annoyed
- Nervous
- Strung out
- Scared
- Suspicious
- Angry
- Confused
- Worried
- Apprehensive
- Crazy
- Terrified
- Uncertain
- Uncomfortable
- Weird
- Exhausted
- Uneasy

In the moment you're feeling all this, however, these convenient labels don't come to you in a neat bullet point list! They arrive all at once, in a great tangled mess, and layered on top of that mess are yet more feelings: You're annoyed with yourself, maybe, or disappointed or concerned about how anxious you feel. You're worried about your nervousness, you're overwhelmed with your irritation, you're annoyed at how weird it all feels . . . On and on it goes.

If you've been battling anxiety for a long time, it may seem completely obvious that the only thing you want is to *not* be anxious anymore. The thought of turning around to face these awful feelings seems insane. Isn't the point to feel better?! The irony, though, is that when you spend a lot of time desperately trying to run away from feelings, you end up knowing very little about what they are and how they work. You may be *emotional* without being emotionally intelligent.

If you label a certain emotion "bad" or "unacceptable," then you immediately stop yourself from processing or understanding it. Judging, invalidating, ignoring, or repressing emotions doesn't make them go away. In fact, wrestling and struggling against "negative emotions" only makes things worse . . .

because the wrestling and struggling are themselves negative emotions.

Now, this isn't the brain teaser that it appears to be on the surface. What's required is that we **reframe the way we think of our emotions entirely**. The old view that sees some emotions as good and some as bad (and in need of fixing as fast as possible) is exactly the kind of mindset that generates more resistance, avoidance, and denial.

But what happens when we stop judging what we feel, and just feel it?

What happens when we stop trying to force or control a situation and instead try to be curious about it and understand it?

How would it change things to imagine that difficult emotions are not enemies but useful messengers?

Throughout this book we will be trying to reframe our attitude toward anxiety itself and all other uncomfortable or unpleasant emotions. The "fix" comes not in finding a way to permanently run away from these uncomfortable feelings, but rather to stay with those feelings and learn to acknowledge, understand, and respect them.

Susan David, a Harvard psychologist and author, explained in her TED Talk how many people either criticize themselves for feeling "negative" emotions or try to suppress those emotions, which only makes them stronger. Avoidance is a fragile and unsustainable position . . . not to mention exhausting. If you've ever tried to force yourself to sit and meditate and found that you felt even more stressed afterward, you'll be familiar with this dynamic. Berating yourself for having the wrong feelings or for not having the right ones is a rigged game, and the only prize you ever seem to win is more anxiety.

Susan David instead emphasizes the importance of emotional agility, rejecting the simplistic notion of emotions as strictly positive or negative. "Negative" emotions hold value, after all. For example, doubt sharpens our analytical thinking, embarrassment can alert us to an important misstep, and anger provides the energy needed to reinforce a violated boundary or assert ourselves.

Fully accepting and experiencing emotions—all of our emotions—is crucial for our mental well-being and leads to better psychological and physical health. Our emotions provide depth, meaning, and color to our experience and are a big part of our decision-making process. If we are unable and unwilling to engage these emotions, we are actually robbing ourselves of a precious source of insight and direction.

This is the attitude behind the concept of *emotions as data, not directives*.

According to Anamaria Nino-Murcia, viewing emotions as data not only alters our perceptions and feelings toward them, but also influences all our subsequent actions, helping us redirect ourselves to more productive responses. Reframing emotions as data liberates people to fully engage with emotions they previously ignored.

- Instead of viewing emotions as permanent, we see them as fleeting and mutable.
- Instead of seeing emotions as evidence of our characters and worth as human beings, we see them as dynamic variables outside ourselves that we can control—i.e., things that can be negotiated, managed, reframed, moderated.
- Instead of seeing emotions as controlling forces we can't resist, we see them simply as information.

If we choose to see emotions as data, we empower ourselves to analyze that data, to process it, and to do something with it. We begin to feel that it is outside of us, and this useful psychological distance allows us to take steps to improve our situation, whatever it is.

A person who is riddled with anxiety is not a person who is experiencing too many "bad emotions"—rather, their problem is that they are not experiencing their emotions in a conscious, effective, or intelligent way. Consider the example of someone lying awake in bed late at night, terrified to death of the monster under the bed. They could spend hours a night, every night, worrying in this way about all the frightening things waiting to get them. Then they could start arguing with themselves, reassuring themselves, chastising themselves for being a big 'fraidy cat. They could buy a self-help book called *Overcoming Your Monster Fear in 30 Days*.

An alternative is to just get up and look. What's under there, anyway? Is it *really* a monster? If it is, well, what kind of monster is it, exactly? What does it want? How did it get under there in the first place? Perhaps you could ask its name and start up a conversation. Maybe you strike a deal with it. Or maybe you could say, "Look, monster, you're cute, but you don't live here. Time to move out." Then you make a note to buy a can of monster-repellent in the morning . . .

It's a silly example, but you get the idea: It's only when we accept, acknowledge, and face our emotions that we give ourselves the opportunity to process them and move forward. If emotions are messengers, then the only real way to make them go away is to listen to them and see what they're trying to tell you. Keep running away, and they keep running after you, trying to pass on that message.

To truly master the problem of anxiety and overthinking, we need to master our own experience, which means becoming more emotionally literate. This is not the same as simply allowing yourself to feel a bunch of vague sensations and be overcome by them. Instead, it's learning how to stand outside of your experience and name it. For this, you'll need a rich and sophisticated emotional vocabulary.

Anamaria Nino-Murcia and her colleague encourage their clients to use this feelings chart:

A Vocabulary of Emotions: I Feel _____

	Happy	Caring	Confident	High/Low Energy	Guilt or Shame	Apathetic	Fearful	Sad	Angry	Uncertain
Mild "A little" "A little bit" "slightly" "mildly"	Glad Pleased Content Warm	Appreciative Grateful Interested in Sympathetic	Committed Competent Determined Focused Open	Calm Chill Laid back Relaxed Serene	Embarrassed Hesitant Reluctant	Disinterested Out Flat	Cautious On edge Shy In a funk Tense Uncomfortable	Disappointed Down Lonely Unhappy	Frustrated Impatient Irritated	Confused Distracted Surprised Unsure
Medium	Cheerful Delighted Optimistic Playful	Admiring Affectionate Close to Compassionate Concerned Empathetic Loving Trusting	Brave Hopeful Proud Receptive Resilient	Awake Eager Excited Lazy Tired Worn out	Apologetic Exposed Guilty Sorry	Aloof Bored Vacant Indifferent	Alarmed Anxious Worried Nervous Scared	Disconnected Discouraged Hurt Insignificant Upset	Annoyed Defensive Exasperated Mad Resentful	Lost Misunderstood Perplexed Stuck
Strong "extremely" "really" "very" "super"	Amazed Ecstatic Elated Overjoyed Thrilled	Adoring Crazy about Fascinated Passionate Protective of Obsessed	Inspired Daring Brash Bold	Enthusiastic Exhausted Fatigued Pumped up	Ashamed Horrible Humiliated Mortified Worthless		Freaked out Horrified Intimidated Terrified	Awful Drained Depressed Hopeless Miserable	Bitter Disgusted Furious Pissed off Outraged Vengeful	Bewildered Overwhelmed Powerless Shocked Stunned

The chart organizes emotions into columns based on related "families," with varying intensity levels along the y-axis. The x-axis depicts a spectrum of emotion families, spanning from positive on the left to negative on the right.

Bear in mind that in this model, the terms "positive" and "negative" emotions refer to the physical sensations they evoke rather than their value or utility. Positive emotions like happiness and caring are associated with comfort and pleasure, while negative emotions like anger, uncertainty, and anxiety induce discomfort. But comfortable or not, emotions are yours, and they're valid. They're real.

Life is change and movement, and so our experiences fluctuate, too, but no emotional experience is inherently better or healthier, just like rain and sunshine both play an important role in an ecosystem.

How to use this chart:

Step 1:

Conduct a quick inventory exercise by circling all the emotions you recall feeling over a specific period. Reflect on whether you expressed those emotions to others, how long they lasted, and what you did with them.

Step 2:
Use the chart over the next two weeks to track your emotions either in real-time or during daily reflection sessions. This allows you to gain more detailed insight into your emotional patterns and fluctuations.

Step 3:
Practice emotional precision. Treat emotional precision as a skill. Instead of vague descriptions like "feeling weird," strive to identify specific emotions like "frustrated, lost, disappointed, and anxious." This richer data enables better understanding and regulation of emotions—and that enables you to take more conscious control of your life through your actions and choices.

Step 4:

Continuously refine your emotional vocabulary by pushing yourself to find more precise words to describe your feelings using the chart. You can add your own shades and nuances as your skill develops. This not only enhances self-awareness but also improves communication with others.

Step 5:
Combine emotional data with deliberate action. Draw conclusions based on your emotion tracker and analyze your triggers. For instance, if your emotions are consistently in the "Uncertain" category, reflect on what is sustaining and feeding that emotion. What emotion is dominant? What tends to come before and after it? Finally, the big question: if this emotion is a messenger, what is it trying to communicate?

Let's say you've been diligently tracking your emotions and notice a recurring pattern of uncertainty cropping up during work meetings. Reflecting on this, you realize that it's often when new projects are introduced or when you're tasked with making important decisions. You zoom in and notice these emotions as emotions. You avoid judging or ignoring them, and you don't immediately launch into "fix it" mode.

Instead, you're strategic and assume that these feelings are valid and mean something. That said, you don't get "hooked" by this feeling, either, or wallow in it. Rather, it's just a data point. You don't like it when you feel that way, no, but you accept that you do. Once you accept it, you start to feel curious, and with some further reflection you understand that you feel most apprehensive when people make demands of you but their instructions are unclear. You realize that your uncertainty is more like a "put on the spot" feeling, and so you decide to make a point of asking for more clarity and information whenever people make these kinds of requests at work.

This feeling, then, had an important message: "You need to communicate a need to your colleagues and make some changes to the way you work." Once heeded, this message disappears, and you no longer feel as uncertain as you did. In fact, you start to really value this unpleasant emotion, because whenever it pops up, it's a helpful sign that you might need to be a bit clearer in asking for direction from others.

Just like any other data point, emotions provide insights into our internal state and the external events that trigger them. Emotions keep you connected to the world and responsive to change. By understanding the relationship between our emotions and the situations that evoke them, we can make more informed choices about how to respond.

Recognize that you are stuck. Understand your emotions as emotions and be curious about how they are functioning and what they point to. Accept it. Ask yourself, "What is the value here?"

Anxiety cannot be shifted by piling more negativity onto it. The best way to work with anxiety is to recognize how you feel and then consciously channel that energy into action that aligns with your goals and values. Performance psychologist Jeremy Adams says it best:

> "What if we could learn to use our emotions as another way of evaluating the world around us? We have many ways of viewing the world and taking in data—from senses, to cognition, to language. But we also have emotions: little packets of semi-autonomous, easily (often independently) activated code. What if, instead of just acting on our emotions when they activate, we're able to notice them, evaluate why they were activated, and integrate that information into our 'decision matrix'?

Could they be another extremely useful data source?"

Three Types of Rumination—and How to Stop

Another name for overthinking is rumination, which actually encompasses a broad range of different behaviors and attitudes. The etymology of the word rumination tells you most of what you need to know: It comes from the Latin *ruminari*, meaning to chew over. It's the word we use for that class of animals that chews the cud, and it describes "passively and repetitively focusing on one's symptoms [. . .] and the possible causes and consequences of these symptoms" (Wells 2004).

Rumination, as defined by the response styles theory (RST, first proposed in 1998 by Nolen-Hoeksema) and the goal progress theory (GPT), involves focused attention on distressing symptoms, their causes, and their consequences, rather than on solutions. Ruminating is not itself an emotion, but rather a style of response to life and its challenges that is associated with emotions like anxiety.

If you're distressed, you may think, "I have a problem with anxiety. I'm too stressed. I worry too much." It may be more useful to think of the situation in terms of what you are actually *doing*, however—and thoughts are a kind of mental action. "I am overthinking right now. I'm returning to the same idea again and again. I'm dwelling on this piece of distressing information."

Rumination can be thought of as a response to a failure to meet or progress toward a goal. Whether that's being rejected, flunking your driver's test, losing money, or arguing with a friend, rumination is a possibility any time we are faced with uncomfortable emotions associated with not getting what we wanted or expected.

As it happens, not all rumination is created equal, and there are actually three proposed forms of rumination:

State Rumination

This form of rumination involves dwelling on the consequences and feelings associated with failure or distress. People who engage in state rumination may focus on the negative emotions and outcomes (states) related to their situation. State rumination is more common in people with pessimistic outlooks, neurotic tendencies, and negative attributional styles. An attributional style is an ingrained way that people explain to themselves why they have had a certain experience, whether positive or negative. A negative attributional style tends to give the same explanation for all events, and it tends to be a bad one—for example, "I'm a victim. The bad things that happen in my life happen because other people are awful."

An example is Dan, who has just had a challenging job interview. The panel asked a few difficult questions at points, and that evening, Dan can't stop thinking about all the stupid things he said and how embarrassed he felt. This is state rumination, as he brings his mind again and again to the feelings of worthlessness and humiliation. Dan is not thinking calmly and rationally about his chances of winning the job, but focusing on how bad he felt at the time.

Action Rumination

Action rumination involves task-oriented thought processes aimed at goal achievement and the correction of mistakes. Instead of passively dwelling on distressing thoughts and feelings, people engaging in action rumination actively seek ways to address their concerns and move closer to their goals. This form of rumination is more constructive and goal-directed compared to state rumination. An example is Clara, who, after a breakup, pours her energy into self-care activities like exercising and seeking therapy to move forward.

Action rumination can take on less healthy forms, though—for example, anxiously Googling symptoms or seeking medical help to fix a perceived illness. This is an attempt to problem-solve that itself may become a problem.

Task-Irrelevant Rumination

Task-irrelevant rumination involves using events or thoughts unrelated to a blocked goal or distressing situation to distract oneself. Rather than directly addressing the problem or focusing on constructive actions, people ruminating this way may engage in unrelated activities or thoughts as a means of temporary escape from the distressing situation. An obvious example is Alex, who is binge-watching TV shows to avoid thinking about a poor exam grade. Alex is "chewing over" things but not in a way that is productive or likely to address the underlying cause of the problem.

There are potentially two other types of rumination, including post-event rumination (painfully rehashing a failed social situation event or situation) and stress-reactive rumination (detailed reviewing of stressful or unpleasant past events and continually interpreting them as worse than they were).

These forms of rumination reflect the different ways in which people may respond to distress or setbacks, with varying levels of effectiveness in addressing the underlying issues. Your rumination may be a blend of several of these. While state rumination may perpetuate negative emotions and hinder problem-solving, action rumination is more able to help you focus on proactive strategies for overcoming obstacles. Task-irrelevant rumination, on the other hand, may offer temporary relief but does not address the root causes of distress.

According to Dr. Greenberg, here are four exercises for compulsive rumination:

Exercise 1: Learn how to interrupt repetitive thoughts

This involves understanding exactly what triggers your rumination and then practicing techniques to stop it. The trick is actively stopping yourself from ruminating whenever you catch yourself doing it—and this is something that gets easier and easier with practice.

Keep track of situations that seem to set off your ruminating mind, and try to identify any patterns or triggers associated with these difficulties. Then you can pre-empt your habit of going down certain mental rabbit holes before they really start.

To make this work, you need plenty of self-awareness, but you don't need Zen-like calm and clarity, just a little curiosity. Get into the habit of asking, "What's going on with me right now?" One trick is to write down your predominant anxious thought on a piece of paper. Name it. Get some psychological distance from it. The next time it pops up for you, try to consciously notice what's happening. "Aha, I'm having that thought again." Realize that you can pick that thought up and put it down again just the same as you can pick up and put down the piece of paper.

For example, you may notice that you often fall into rumination when waiting for someone to respond to a text. You notice a pattern that always starts with the thought, "What if I said something offensive?" But because you have noticed this thought, you're more able to recognize it each time it comes up. The next time someone doesn't respond quickly to a text, and you notice yourself beginning to ruminate, just think, "Oh, here's that same old thought again. I'm just not going to go there." Then, you may decide to put your attention elsewhere or distract yourself.

Interrupt negative thoughts by consciously imagining yourself yelling STOP mentally, or deliberately standing up and moving around to cut short a train of thought. Forcefully imagine that your mind is a train and that you can pull a lever to switch tracks. Think of something else you're excited about, make plans, laugh it off, do something physical, or simply decide then and there that you won't "take the bait" and start ruminating.

Practice Switching between Rumination and Non-rumination Intentionally

Once you get better at interrupting your own automatic thoughts, you can try deliberately switching your own attention onto and off of certain thoughts. This exercise helps you gain control over your thought patterns and can be incredibly empowering. You'll engage in short bursts of rumination followed by longer periods of intentionally not ruminating. The idea is that if you can switch the rumination tap on, then you can switch it off! The goal is to make this switching process feel more natural over time and to convince yourself that rumination is not some supernaturally powerful force that you can never resist. In fact, engaging your ability to control your experience this way only strengthens it, like exercising a muscle.

For example, you may be ruminating over something embarrassing you did, and your mind keeps returning to the awful feelings of shame and humiliation you felt. Let's say you tell yourself, "Okay, I'm going to deliberately ruminate for the next minute," and then that's what you do. Maybe you try to ruminate as hard as you can! After a minute, you stop yourself. Importantly, you are not practicing how to ruminate, but practicing how to consciously *stop* when you want to. How does it feel to tell your mind, "That's enough now"? What works best?

Use a timer and practice this exercise when you are feeling relatively unrushed and calm. The length of time doesn't matter as much as the ease with which you are able to start and stop—i.e., how well you are able to self-control. Keep going and notice if and how you are improving. Do a few of these "reps" every day and you will not only build your self-control, but you will also convince yourself that there is nothing especially scary or out-of-control about certain ways of thinking. If you catch yourself ruminating, just stop. That's all.

Create Your Own "Exposure Therapy"

Recall that a big part of anxious rumination is a tendency to avoid and escape certain unpleasant emotions. Turn this around by strategically facing your rumination triggers. Again, this is something to attempt once you're more comfortable with starting and stopping your rumination at will. We'll consider exposure therapy in more detail in a later chapter.

For now, just practice setting specific times to intentionally expose yourself to triggering stimuli for brief periods, then practice *not* engaging with the temptation to ruminate. Sometimes, when you ruminate, you are in a reactive state of mind and simply responding to stimuli. If you deliberately seek out a triggering situation, however, you are the one in control. It may feel scary to face certain thoughts and feelings, but remember that the goal here is not to needlessly upset yourself, but rather to start gathering evidence that you are in control and can decide whether to ruminate or not. That's why it's crucial that this exercise is premeditated—it's no longer exposure if you catch yourself mid-rumination!

You might learn over the course of a few weeks to actively turn your rumination on and off. You next decide to practice turning rumination off in the presence of a stimulus you already know triggers you. For example, you might notice that certain kinds of news stories on certain topics tend to trigger a spiral of rumination about your finances, making you worry endlessly about money. Being aware of this, you selectively expose yourself to that kind of news story, then pause. You notice what you're feeling and thinking. From there, you try to calm yourself down and turn that rumination off while still in the presence of that news story. You practice for a few minutes, then do something else. The next day, you try again and notice that the news story, while upsetting, doesn't seem to trigger you quite so much, and so on.

There isn't necessarily any value in "toughening" yourself up or learning to endure unpleasant sensations just for the sake of it. Rather, the goal is to build your own self-control and self-awareness and become skilled at directing and managing your own experience, rather than passively allowing it to control you.

Confront Ongoing Triggers without Allowing Yourself to Engage in Rumination

In this final exercise, you take things even further. Try to see if you can face certain situations and triggers without rumination at all. This could involve holding a knife without imagining harm, reading about challenging topics without getting caught up in obsessive thoughts, or looking at triggering images without analyzing or seeking reassurance. You'll have to be creative and structure your exercises in a way that comfortably challenges the kind of rumination you most tend to fall into.

Gradually progress to handling more prolonged triggers once you've mastered dealing with brief triggers. The goal is to demonstrate that you can manage ongoing triggers without succumbing to obsessive thoughts or compulsions. So, you may gradually find that you are able to read a distressing news story without even *starting* a rumination spiral in the first place.

You'll notice that the above exercises are the opposite of what some of us do when attempting to manage anxiety and overthinking. When faced with uncomfortable sensations, the tendency may be to escape and avoid, but in the long term, this gives the thing we are avoiding too much power over us. Avoiding stimuli might feel like it helps initially, but in the long run, we are so much less resilient. Think of it not as an exercise in making anxiety smaller, but in making yourself much bigger than the anxiety.

Adjust Your Assumptions

Our ingrained assumptions, core beliefs, expectations, biases, and personal narratives can all influence our overthinking habits and our anxiety levels. What core beliefs may be sabotaging you?

Ben is a young engineering student who is stressed and overwhelmed with his life. He is starting to have trouble sleeping, he is forgetting things and procrastinating too much, and he has started to notice that he is snappy and irritable with friends. Recently, he's become obsessed with the idea that he has a serious but undiagnosed mental health issue. Ever since watching a news segment on OCD, he's wondered if he could have the condition. Does he need treatment? Can he be helped? What's wrong with him, anyway? Why is he like this? Can people tell? He spends hours online in the evening "researching" his self-diagnosed condition.

Ben has a problem, but it's not the one he thinks he has. From Ben's perspective, there is something badly wrong with him, and whatever it is, the thing is one hundred percent out of his control, and he is at its mercy. Part of him realizes that the way he is currently living is not healthy or sustainable, but the way he is framing the problem is itself part of the problem.

For Ben, the issue is that he is fatally flawed and somehow inferior. His "solution" is to try to find out what that is.

The real issue, however, is not that there is something fatally flawed and inferior about him, but that he has fully bought into the idea of his own inferiority without recognizing that this is just an *assumption*, not a fact.

Many people spend years of their lives "working on" a problem in therapy that they don't actually have. This is because they ask themselves questions like "Why am I such a loser?" or "How can I deal with the fact that everyone hates me?" but never examine the deeply held assumptions that make them ask those questions in the first place.

Ben may find that relentlessly seeking a diagnosis (or even receiving one!) doesn't help much. What does help is challenging his assumptions that he is somehow worse than everyone else, or that his struggles and challenges are uniquely awful compared to other people's.

In his book *Think Better Thoughts*, author Thibaut Meurisse suggests that our internal dialogue, or the story we tell ourselves, plays a significant role in shaping our lives and determining our success or failure. While many people may recognize that they are not achieving their desired outcomes, they may fail to identify the underlying disempowering thoughts that contribute to this situation. These disempowering thoughts are deeply ingrained beliefs that influence their perceptions, behaviors, and ultimately, their results. If we wish to "get better," we need to direct our attention here, to the stories we tell, and not get caught up in the stories themselves.

Thibaut calls these stories "meta-assumptions." These grand narratives represent overarching beliefs that underpin a multitude of disempowering thoughts. By identifying these meta-assumptions, you can gain insight into the root cause of certain limiting behaviors (like overthinking) and begin to challenge and overcome them.

"I am not enough."

This is the idea that you are inadequate in some way—i.e., not good, smart, attractive, young, educated, or strong enough to do what you'd like to do.

You'll know you have made this assumption if you have "imposter syndrome" or simply assume that any success is a fluke or mistake. This core belief will show up as any story that explains events and people's behavior in terms of your own lack. For example, "They didn't hire me. They must think I'm an idiot."

"I don't have enough/there isn't enough."

This is the belief that you personally lack resources, time, money, etc., but also that there is a general shortage of resources in the world, and that there isn't enough for everybody. This core belief may show up as competitiveness, rushing, zero-sum thinking, jealousy, suspicion, and judgment for others and yourself. "I have to get him before he gets me."

"I'm powerless."

This is the belief that who you are and what you do is insignificant. This is a passive, disempowered core belief that manifests as a conviction that the course of your life is determined by powerful outside forces. It can also lead to blame, a victim mentality, and an unwillingness to accept the role you play in creating your experience. "Life is so unfair. I can't be happy today because of the rotten childhood I've had. Nothing can be done about it now."

"I'm a slave to my emotions."

This is when you overidentify with your emotions and let them define you, or else see them as irresistible and non-negotiable directives that control you (see the previous chapter!). Sadly, this is a core belief that a lot of self-help ends up reinforcing. While it's always good to acknowledge your emotions, they are not the entirety of your being. "Well, I have depression and anxiety, so I always do such-and-such." This is just another way of saying, "I have no agency to create my own life."

"I'm better than others" or "Others are better than me."

This is when you see yourself as superior/inferior to other people. Some people can feel both and swing wildly between narcissism and shame. This can lead to unrealistic expectations ("everyone should like me and it's a problem if someone doesn't" or "I should stay in this abusive relationship because it's all I deserve"). It's also a core belief that keeps your focus on yourself, rather than on your goals out there in the world, and the concrete steps you could take to achieve those goals. Over-personalizing things (i.e., making yourself the eternal reference point, either positively or negatively) is closely associated with anxiety and rumination.

"I'm self-aware."

This is the belief you know yourself well when, in fact, you ignore many things about yourself. We can only correct what we are able to acknowledge isn't working in the first place. If we wrongly assume that all our current assumptions are correct, we may be skirting close to denial. This is the person who says, "My gut is telling me that I shouldn't apply for the job, and I always trust my gut," when in reality they are just fearful of taking a risk and are passing off anxious and avoidant behavior as something more enlightened.

"Success is outside of my control."

This is the idea that success is always going to be inaccessible to you because you lack resources, talent, money, etc. It's the deep belief that success is just not a part of your identity and is something that belongs to others but not you. This so-called "external locus of control" is one that undervalues your own agency and responsibility and takes you out of the driver's seat of your own lives. It may look like waiting for others to give you permission to pursue your dreams, or overvaluing other people's validation. It can also look like wanting magic bullets and overnight success: "I'll never sort out my life . . . unless I win the lottery!"

Earlier on, we considered the idea that emotions can be thought of as data. Our beliefs and automatic assumptions can be understood in the same way. When we recognize our thoughts *as thoughts*, and our beliefs *as beliefs*, then we give ourselves the opportunity to question them, adjust them, fine-tune them ... or sometimes get rid of them entirely!

The trouble is when we simply assume that what we think and believe is automatically true. We take our own word for it. It's perfectly normal to make assumptions and to create stories to help us understand the world around us. While having rules is essential for making sense of the world and functioning effectively, the type of rules we adhere to is crucial. Helpful rules are realistic, flexible, and adaptable, enabling us to function healthily and safely. They should earn their keep—i.e., when they are no longer useful or accurate, we need to be able to replace them with thoughts and ideas that are.

No one can control everything in life, and few of us have perfect knowledge about every situation we find ourselves in. But that's precisely why we need flexibility in our thinking. The stories we tell can then be used as tools to help us live the life we want to live. On the other hand, unhelpful assumptions are unrealistic, unreasonable, and rigid. Not only are they not useful or accurate, but they also actively get in the way of us living the life we want to live.

Psychologist Albert Ellis was an early founder of cognitive behavioral therapy, and he had an amusing term for the kind of inflexible and unrealistic thinking that hindered people the most; he called it "musterbation." He claimed that people suffered when they held rigid expectations and inflexible demands on reality. Their problem was not that reality didn't live up to these expectations, but rather the expectations themselves.

In Ben's case, the story he is telling himself may come with a whole series of "must" and "shouldn't" rules: "I must do well at college or else; I mustn't ever feel stressed or unhappy; I shouldn't ever fail; I can't ask for help; if I am meant to be an engineer then I shouldn't have this much trouble with the course . . ."

Of course, sometimes our assumptions are correct. But we can only know this for sure if we are able to become aware of our assumptions *as assumptions* and put them to the test. Could there be one or more unfounded assumptions at the core of your overthinking and anxiety?

Step 1: Identify an unhelpful rule, assumption, or core belief that impacts your life. Reflect on its impact on you. Is it helpful? Is it accurate? Is it kind? Evaluating the effects of these rules and assumptions is crucial for understanding their influence on your life.

Step 2: Start to notice when and where this assumption pops up, and consider where it came from. What has sustained it over time? Is this "rule" still even relevant?

Step 3: Consider the unreasonableness of the rule or assumption by assessing its inflexibility and rigidity. Acknowledge that these rules may not align with the realities of the world or your current circumstances as an adult. Reflect on how these rules may have made sense in the past, and what they protected you from. Are you different today from when you first decided to live by this rule?

Step 4: Consider the drawbacks of adhering to the rule or assumption by evaluating its impact on your life. Assess whether the advantages are genuine and outweigh the disadvantages. Reflect on how the rule may limit opportunities, hinder enjoyment, diminish achievements, strain relationships, or impede progress toward life goals. Compare these disadvantages with the advantages previously identified. If the disadvantages outweigh the benefits, consider developing a more balanced rule.

Step 5: Use less extreme language and consider alternative perspectives to create a more adaptable and sophisticated rule. Look for "must" and "have to" and rephrase these ideas to include more grey area. If crafting a new rule feels challenging, just experiment with it for a trial period. See how the new thought impacts your feelings and behavior. Can you find evidence for this updated belief?

Step 6: The last step involves implementing your new rule and assumption into your daily life. This step is crucial because your old rule has influenced your behavior for some time, and adopting a new perspective requires aligning your actions accordingly. By practicing new behaviors, you allow the new rule to become ingrained in your new belief system, fostering positive changes in your mindset and actions over time. The following worksheet can help you keep track of these reflections:

Improving

Adjusting the Rules

Rule and/or assumption I would like to adjust
What impact has this rule (and/or assumption) had on my life?
How do I know this rule is in operation?
Where did this rule (and/or assumption) come from?
In what ways is this rule (and/or assumption) unreasonable?

Advantages of this Rule	Disadvantages of this Rule

What is an alternative rule (and/or assumption) that is more balanced and flexible?
What can I do to put this rule (and/or assumption) into practice on a daily basis?

Module 7: Adjusting Rules & Assumptions

Summary:

- Chronic and habitual overthinking can damage relationships, interfere with work, and utterly exhaust you in the process. Thankfully, it can be changed, and the first step is awareness of our emotions, and the acknowledgment that these emotions are *data and not directives*. This way, we empower ourselves to analyze that data, process it, and do something useful with it.
- Emotions are neither good nor bad; it's only when we accept all of our

experience and acknowledge and face our emotions that we give ourselves the opportunity to process them and move forward. We need emotional literacy and to label our feelings.

- Emotions are valid and have value as messengers, but you need to understand emotions *as emotions*.
- Rumination means passively and repetitively focusing on symptoms, causes, and consequences, but not on solutions. It can be thought of as a response to a failure to meet or progress toward a goal and has three types according to its focus: state, task, or irrelevant task.
- To overcome rumination, it's important to consciously interrupt unhelpful thought trains—identify triggers and recurrent patterns and stop/distract yourself when rumination threatens to start. Try intentionally switching between rumination and non-rumination and practice your own "exposure therapy." Eventually, the goal is to confront ongoing triggers without engaging in rumination.
- Our ingrained assumptions, core beliefs, expectations, biases, and personal narratives can all influence our overthinking habits and our

anxiety levels. Re-appraise your metanarratives about yourself, your life, and your anxiety. Unhelpful assumptions are unrealistic, unreasonable, and rigid, and they get in the way of us living the life we want to live.

Chapter 2: Find Clarity

Have you ever felt like your mind was quite literally a tangle of words? Like a thousand people all talking at once, or a million complicated threads all knotted together? Oh, and everything is also racing at one hundred miles an hour?

This feeling of overwhelm is extremely common with anxiety and overthinking. The trouble is that our attempts to get out of this tangle often make it worse—we end up thinking more, stressing more, tensing more. What is the way out?

In the previous chapter, we briefly mentioned the phenomenon of **psychological distance** and how useful it can be to see your own thoughts, feelings, and beliefs as somewhat separate from yourself, rather than fusing with them so completely that they become a defining and all-encompassing part of your reality. This is one surefire way to bring a little more clarity to your experience.

The clarity we can find is not necessarily the clarity that comes with having a completely calm and quiet mind, but rather the clarity that comes from being able to step away from the noise for a little while. In this chapter, we'll explore a few ways to do that.

Unload with Freewriting

Freewriting or "brain dumping" involves unloading any thoughts, anxieties, to-do lists, and emotions onto paper to alleviate stress and free up mental space. It's a form of therapeutic writing that can help manage overwhelming thoughts and emotions by releasing them onto the page. When that anxious, tangled chaos is out there on the page, it can feel as though it's not so much *in here* anymore. It's easier to deal with. Brain dumps are similar to other types of journaling, offering benefits such as improved mental health and reduced anxiety.

Research suggests that regular journaling, including brain dumping, can lead to decreased anxiety and stress, increased resilience, and improved sleep quality. There are no strict rules for brain dumping; it can be done as frequently as desired, with the duration determined by your own individual preference. Regular practice (that means a few times a week) is recommended for the greatest benefits.

Here are some steps to getting started:

Set a Freewriting Schedule

Choose a time of day that works best for you to engage in freewriting. Some people prefer to do it in the morning to clear their minds for the day ahead, while others find it helpful after work to decompress. Some may prefer to brain dump at night before bed so that they can release all tensions and worries that accumulated over the day and have a peaceful night's sleep. Experiment to find a time that suits you best.

Write Down EVERY Idea in Any Language or Format You Prefer

Start by writing down every idea that comes to mind about your topic, regardless of how "crazy" or irrelevant it may seem. Don't judge your ideas at this stage, and remember that no one else will see your freewriting. Don't worry about grammar or spelling, and keep reminding yourself that you are not trying to produce anything in particular; rather, it's about the experience of writing it down. If perfectionism is a problem, you might like to experiment with completely destroying your notes once you're done with them.

Continue for Fifteen to Twenty Minutes

Keep freewriting for a set amount of time, usually fifteen to twenty minutes, or until you feel you have enough material to start working on (in the next section, we'll take a closer look at what to do with the notes). The more material you have, the easier it is to start spotting recurrent patterns and themes. That said, do not feel you have to keep writing and writing if you have put down everything you need to and the fifteen minutes is not yet over.

Freewriting is a wonderful way to build self-awareness and fine-tune your emotional vocabulary. It helps you slow down, calm down, and pay attention. There are a few caveats, though. Anxious people have a special talent for turning everything—even a stress-management technique—into another method for stressing! There is no real way to do it wrong, but try to avoid pausing and going back to read what you wrote before the twenty-minute period is over. Just keep your hand moving and don't look back.

You don't have to be good or impressive, or write something earth-shattering or insightful. You can choose to write in bullet points, full paragraphs, or barely legible scribbles. You can write about what's bugging you today or something more general about your life. What occurs to you the moment you put the pen to paper? Write about *that*, and write without self-censoring. When you're done, remember to put a date on the entry.

Once you've gathered a few entries, you'll probably start noticing patterns. What language do you tend to use again and again? What ideas, assumptions, thoughts, feelings, themes, beliefs, and problems repeatedly crop up? What comes before and after these feelings? How long do they typically last, and what is it that makes some moods shift?

Structured Stress Relief Diary Procedure

Freewriting is a more open-ended, loose way to "take your emotional temperature" and start teasing out broader patterns and cycles in your own life. But you can also take a more structured approach, or even do a mix of both structured and open-ended. Try the following procedure to begin gathering useful data about exactly what overthinking and anxiety looks like in your life:

1. Make regular entries in your stress diary throughout the day, noting the

date and time of each entry. Record any stressful incidents you experience or encounter, providing details about the event.
2. Assess your current happiness level subjectively on a scale of zero to ten, with zero being the unhappiest and ten being the happiest. Describe the mood you're experiencing alongside this rating (use an emotions chart or wheel to help you find the right word to describe what you're feeling).
3. Subjectively assess how effectively you're working on a scale of zero to ten, where zero signifies complete ineffectiveness and ten indicates peak effectiveness. Reflect on your productivity level and any challenges you're facing in completing tasks. Try to do this without shame and judgment; just stay curious and neutral and try to understand what is happening.
4. Clearly identify the fundamental cause of the stress you're experiencing, maintaining honesty and objectivity. Document any physical or emotional symptoms you're feeling in response to the stressors. If you are already becoming familiar with your core beliefs and assumptions, note them when you spot them.

5. Reflect on how well you handled the stressful event and whether your reaction helped to resolve the problem or exacerbated it. You can explore the outcome of different responses over time—do you still feel the same about certain events ten minutes, a day, or a week later?
6. Review your stress diary entries to identify the most frequent and unpleasant stressors. Analyze the underlying causes of these stressors and assess how effectively you handled them. Identify patterns in the situations that cause you stress and brainstorm potential solutions to improve these circumstances.

This is the ideal format, but feel free to customize it.

Date and Time	Most Recent Stressful Event Experienced	How Happy Do You Feel Now? (Scale 0-10)	Your Current Mood	How Effectively Are You Working Now? (0-10)	Fundamental Cause of the Event	How Stressed Do You Feel Now? (Scale 0-10)	Physical Symptom During Stressful Event	How Well Did You Handle the Event?

Organize Your Overwhelmed Mind with Anxiety Mapping

A great way to get a handle on overthinking is to get organized and learn to make your mind work *for* you, rather than *against* you. Worrying and overthinking can be addictive. That's because it can be so difficult to draw a clear line between "useful thinking" and "harmful thinking." It's especially difficult because the only way you can find out the difference is to, well, think some more.

It's a little like being addicted to food. Eating in itself is a healthy, normal behavior. It's more than that—it's crucial to your survival. Eating too much or all the wrong things, however, can become unhealthy and abnormal. Eating incorrectly can start to seriously undermine your survival.

In the same way, thinking in itself is not a problem. The human mind is a wonderous adaptation that has allowed our species to achieve a level of development unrivaled by any other. The human brain is arguably the most complex and sophisticated organ in the known universe and has made possible feats of creation, problem-solving, and growth that have literally changed the world.

But such a powerful tool incorrectly used can obviously work against us. Thinking "too much" or "incorrectly" has far wider consequences for our lives than a malfunctioning appetite. An addiction to overthinking can take our best tools—the ability to evolve, to create, to analyze, to predict, and all the rest—and turns them against us.

In this section, we're going to explore a method for rescuing all the good things that come with thinking from the muddle and chaos of *over*thinking. The anxious mind is a little like an overgrown vegetable garden or a wild and unruly horse. If you can carefully and strategically prune back the weeds, and if you can tame and train the horse, then you are deriving the fullest potential from both.

The solution to overthinking, then, is not "underthinking" or forcing yourself not to think of anything (we will certainly explore mindfulness techniques and meditation in a later chapter, but this is absolutely *not* the same as "not thinking"). Rather, the solution to overthinking is to cultivate *better thinking*. Prune the weeds, train the horse.

The good news is that, as an anxious overthinker, you already possess the power necessary to think well. What you may lack is the focus, discipline, and intention that channels all that power into something useful.

Mind mapping is a technique that can help you learn to better channel and train your thinking. This is a technique that organizes thoughts into a structured and easily understandable design, akin to purposefully connected links in a chain. Unlike the chaotic tangle of overthinking, mind mapping allows thoughts to flow seamlessly, interlinked yet organized. Most importantly, mind maps are *purposive*—they don't go round and round in circles, achieving nothing. They are instead intentional and have direction. There's a point to them.

Overthinkers have the habit of overstimulating themselves, but we also happen to live in a world soaked in an abundance of information—much of it irrelevant—and countless forces trying to catch and harness our attention for their own purposes. Achieving clarity through mind mapping can feel like discovering an oasis in a desert of overwhelming thoughts, whether that desert is one of your own creation or something the world imposes on you from the outside.

Overthinking is the process of excessively and recklessly analyzing situations, often with regret or worry about the past or future. It can lead to mental health issues like anxiety and depression, hinder productivity, strain relationships, and impact overall well-being—the opposite of what your mind is supposed to be doing for you. Consistent negative thought patterns can result in paralysis by analysis, misunderstandings in relationships, and even physical symptoms such as insomnia and fatigue. Understanding overthinking is crucial for addressing it, with one effective technique being mind mapping.

Mind mapping is a visualization technique that mirrors the natural flow and structure of ideas in the human brain. Unlike linear lists or chaotic arrays of thoughts, mind maps offer a centralized, organized, and hierarchical representation of concepts, making them easier to comprehend, recall, and utilize. Originating from Tony Buzan's teachings in the 1960s, mind mapping has evolved into a powerful cognitive tool beyond mere notetaking, serving as a method for brainstorming, problem-solving, and decision-making.

A specific version of mind mapping is the anxiety map. Creating and assessing an anxiety map involves the process of organizing and reflecting on the thoughts and beliefs contributing to stress. In the previous section we practiced "brain dumps" and getting chaotic information out of our minds and onto the page. From there we gave ourselves the opportunity to start processing the patterns and themes we discovered.

Anxiety maps extend this practice. Sometimes you're overthinking about something complexly pointless and wasting your time. But sometimes there is a legitimate and useful thread of reasoning hiding somewhere inside the mess of overthinking. An anxiety mind map can help you turn a stressful mess into something you can actually use to improve your life.

The big idea behind such a map is to reduce the complexity of thoughts, cut out what's irrelevant, and find a way to organize and streamline the content *toward some end*. If the idea is to condense and simplify, then it can be a good thing to force your unruly thoughts in a single word, image, sentence, or symbol, and then move on. Traditionally, they were created with pen and paper, but now there are plenty of free and paid tools that offer advantages such as unlimited space and easy modification. There is also something liberating, however, about the permanence of ink once it is put down on paper.

This process also allows for clarity when confronted with unfamiliar or overwhelming emotions. The mind map essentially helps you take a scalpel to all your experiences and separate out thoughts from feelings, facts from perceptions, and reality from your experiences of reality.

A mind map has the following features:

A central idea—Written down and circled, occupying the center of the page. It's the heart of the matter. This can be a problem, an upcoming event, a goal, or a decision.

Branches—Extending from the central idea are related subcategories and themes. These are major divisions.

Secondary branches—Extending out from these, like branches of a tree, are smaller and smaller subdivisions representing a structured hierarchy of related ideas.

Visual elements—A good mind map represents the underlying structure of a thinking process with words, but also with color, size, symbols, proportions, images, and relative position. Use these features as a shorthand to communicate relationships, relative importance, priorities, etc.

Now, if you read the above, you may be thinking, "But how on earth will I know what the central idea is? I'm overthinking precisely because I don't know how any of these things connect to one another!" Well, it's by creating the mind map that we uncover these things for ourselves. This is why you shouldn't try too hard to make your mind map pretty or final—you may end up creating many iterative versions before you find the clarity you're looking for.

The mind map is not a snapshot of what is already in our head—after all, that's just like a ball of tangled threads, right? Instead, the mind map's power comes from the effort we make to construct it. It's like taking that ball of threads and gradually picking them apart, laying them flat, and seeing which one connects to which. The process is exploratory *and* creative. We are finding out what's there, but we are also imposing our will and making more deliberate the connections and structures that we wish to be there.

To create your own mind map, try the following:

1. Begin with a central idea. This should be fairly obvious—what's at the top of your mind? For example, you may write "Should I leave my job?" which represents a recurrent stressful topic of rumination for you. You could also write "Mom's cancer" or "Public speaking terror" to represent different issues, goals, or problems.

2. Create the branches. You want to let your thoughts flow freely, as with brain dumping, but remember that you are trying to tease out main themes. Perhaps, in ruminating about whether to leave your job or not, you identify three main aspects: financial worries, overall work satisfaction, and vague, more personal feelings associated with your current role.
3. Dig deeper by adding sub-branches. Now, tackle each branch separately. Let's say you look at "financial worries." What are the components of this aspect of your anxiety? If you find your mind wandering off to think about other unrelated ideas, bring it back to fully explore the current branch first. Let's say you add a few sub-branches: You want a new job, but you're concerned that nobody will pay you as much as the current job does, and you are separately worried about your lack of savings. Perhaps you notice that you have recurring thoughts of shame, fear of failure, and irritation with a particular work colleague, but you slow down and deliberately untangle that from the current thread.
4. Keep going. Use plenty of visual elements as necessary. Make sure that

you are creating a structure—how are the elements related to one another? Is there a hierarchy? Can some points be eliminated? Can some points be combined? Can you identify any cause-and-effect relationships? Any reinforcing loops or points of particular anxiety?

When you are done, you should have a clear picture of your anxiety. Note, this is not a picture of a *solution*—just a picture of the current situation as it stands.

Now what? You can use your mind map to inspire strategic action. In our example, you might untangle your problem and eventually discover that you don't have a job problem at all, but rather that your primary source of anxiety is a lack of financial clarity. This naturally suggests a few ways forward—i.e., goals you can set for yourself. Perhaps you decide to face a few unpleasant financial truths you've been avoiding, sign up for a financial literacy class, or sit down to make a revised budget that will give you a better sense of your long-term financial goals.

This is the value of a mind map. You are not meant to stay dwelling on the tangle for too long, but you should find a clear way to the next step. Often, sitting down to create a mind map reveals new dimensions to the problem you would not have perceived otherwise. Sometimes, the big insight is that there isn't really a problem in the first place!

A mind map can sometimes help you identify your priorities—i.e., there may be a lot to think about, but all you can do is focus on your next move, and then your next one. This brings clarity but also relief, since you stop thinking about a million things at once and just think about the next thing in a linear series. If you're trying to make a decision, a mind map can help you stay focused and create objective lists of pros and cons or explore possible outcomes without getting derailed by irrelevant thoughts and ideas.

With overthinking, it can sometimes be a surprise to discover just how much of the tangle of thoughts is repetition—in other words, the tangle looks chaotic but is really just the same thought repeated in different forms. A mind map can help you quieten all this down and collapse it into one thought. This frees up space on your mind map and in your mind!

As you practice this kind of mental decluttering and organization, you are continually reinforcing the idea that it is you who is in control. You can always stop, become aware, and get some distance from these thoughts. Your mind map isn't set in stone, and you can always return to it and revise it as you go along. In fact, if you have created many mind maps, you give yourself a longitudinal view on your own anxiety, which can be very valuable. You may notice emergent patterns over time and certain broader themes.

By identifying and naming these themes, you are so much less caught up in them when they arise. For example, you may notice over the course of a few months that you have a tendency to want to quit and run away from things whenever the tension of avoiding unpleasant truths gets to be too much. You first notice this dynamic when creating a mind map for work, but months later notice that you do a similar thing in your relationships, and later again when it comes to achieving a lifelong goal. In other words, the insight you gain from a single mind map can have cumulative benefits and help you build self-awareness that lasts long after the original anxiety has passed.

Turn Off Those False Alarms

One final way to cut down on the noise and chaos of overthinking is to get real about your worries—i.e., *how much of what you are perceiving as a threat is genuinely a threat?* This question alone could drastically cut down on mental noise.

Imagine that one day, your partner seems a little distant and distracted. A thought pops into your head: "They're pulling away. They're falling out of love with me. Maybe I did something wrong..."

Your brain has drawn your attention to a possible threat to your well-being. Instantly, you turn all your focus onto this threat. Could it be true? You try to think of ways to reduce the harm, to protect yourself, to solve the problem. You get stuck assessing and reassessing the risk, dreaming up even more threats to come... Before you know it, you're trapped in a horrible tunnel of anxious overthinking.

Originally, the anxiety response evolved in humans to protect them. The five senses provide information about the environment, and the brain puts all that information together. It constantly monitors the environment, and if something looks potentially threatening, a biological and cognitive response is initiated. This is a good thing—it's what helps you identify potential problems, pre-empt danger, adapt, survive, and cope. Without this alarm system, you'd be dead.

Prolonged anxiety, rumination, worry, and overthinking, however, are what results when the alarm system is overactive and gives so many false positives that it starts to be a problem in itself. Anxiety and overthinking can be understood as manifestations of the misfunctioning of this warning system. When anxiety is activated, people narrow their focus onto potential threats, but this narrowed focus comes with disadvantages, such as wrongly interpreting ambiguous situations as harmful ones.

This narrowed attention can lead to exaggerated perceptions of danger, perpetuating a cycle of worry and rumination. In our example, your anxiety loop may lead you to conclude with one hundred percent certainty that your partner is about to leave you at any moment . . . when they did little more than sit on the sofa and stare noncommittally out the window. The brain's inherent bias toward perceiving and prioritizing threats further fuels overthinking, as people overestimate the likelihood and severity of negative outcomes while underestimating their ability to cope.

False alarms are common occurrences driven by the brain's tendency to misjudge situations, misread others' intentions, and misinterpret internal sensations. This is because perceived threats are often based on predictions, leading to an overestimation of the likelihood or severity of future threats due to uncertainty.

Throughout life, the brain learns and remembers what is threatening through both conscious and non-conscious processes, such as fear conditioning in the amygdala. Unfortunately, these threat associations can persist and generalize to situations that are not actually dangerous. Perhaps in the past you had emotionally distant partners who broke up with you out of the blue. Even without obvious prior conditioning, the propensity for false alarms is considered a natural feature of the brain's threat response system and has evolved to prioritize safety in ambiguous or potentially risky situations. But that doesn't mean that we get no say in the process! It certainly doesn't mean that we have to passively go along with every false alarm.

If, to return to our example, we notice our partner being a little distant, we can instead recognize this as a false alarm. Instead of looking around for the proverbial fire and worrying ourselves sick about how we're going to escape the building and what we'll take with us and how bad it might feel to have third-degree burns, we stop and acknowledge that the fire alarm may simply be wrong. There is no fire. Therefore, there is no need to engage with the alarm. In our example, this may mean reminding yourself that your partner has not actually said or done anything, and that there really is zero indication of a threat.

Anxiety is an inaccurate perception of threat. Any time you are anxiously overthinking, it's often because your mind has wrongly predicted that something bad will happen in the future. It's a question of perception and perspective. To combat anxiety, we need two broad skills: First, the presence of mind to be able to stop and consider what is happening to us, and second, to more objectively evaluate the threat. It may feel like the sky is falling, but usually, it isn't. Stop. Breathe. Look around. You have time to evaluate, and when you do, you may discover that you perceived way more threat than there actually was.

A lot of this prediction and appraisal happens automatically and outside of your awareness. It may seem very real and obvious to you, but remind yourself that these are learned and conditioned behaviors. Your "intuition" is often nothing more than a habit. A conscious part of your brain, however, can override these automatic conditioned habits and steer your experience, as long as you are giving yourself enough time to become mindful of what is happening.

Along with overestimating threat, you may also be underestimating your own ability to cope—or discounting it entirely. This makes for a dangerous combination: "Something totally awful is going to happen . . . and I will not be able to stand it." You may be so focused on the idea of the awful thing happening that you forget just how well you have handled things just like it in the past. But you *can* endure and survive hardship. In your ruminations, you may imagine yourself as powerless and at the mercy of catastrophic forces much bigger than you. You may forget that you will face any challenge in your life with a set of coping strategies and resources, just as you always have.

False Alarm or "Intuition"?

At some point, you can't quite decide how accurate your appraisal of threat really is. What if your partner really *is* plotting to leave you? What if you really *did* have cancer all along? Let's be honest: Life absolutely does contain threats, dangers, disappointments, and pains.

This is not the complex puzzle it seems to be, however. There are ways to accurately appraise threat, and even if we do occasionally lack enough information to make that appraisal, we are always at liberty to say, "I don't really know right now." Yes, it is always an option to refrain from making a judgment call! Use the following questions to help discern between a genuine alarm and a false alarm:

What *exactly* is the perceived threat that is causing your anxiety right now? Be precise and put a label on it. Big fears are often just vague fears, and they shrink down to a more realistic size once put into words.

Being as neutral and objective as possible, **how likely is this threat to actually happen?** Remember that an outcome can feel one hundred percent absolutely terrifying to contemplate while still having a very low chance of happening.

If the threat did happen, how bad would it really be? Be honest if you're catastrophizing. A bad outcome may mean discomfort, embarrassment, disappointment, and so on without it being a full-blown disaster. Be careful to distinguish between inconvenience/unpleasantness and *harm* (note also that there isn't really a point in asking this question if you've already determined that the threat is highly unlikely).

Think back to previous situations like this one. **How did you handle things in the past?** This question will counter the tendency toward narrowed attention and remind you of your strengths and ability to cope.

Finally, if this is a risky and scary situation, is doing it anyway going to help you create a more meaningful life for yourself? In other words, **is engaging with the threat actually worth it?** When your alarm system is activated, this question may seem like the furthest thing from your mind. But there is sometimes reward in risk. Let your values guide those decisions, and not your fears.

Four Steps to Calm

Dr. Jeffrey M. Schwartz from the UCLA School of Medicine advocates for bio-behavioral treatment to retrain the brain stuck in OCD thought patterns. This approach, while challenging, offers longer-lasting and more effective results compared to relying solely on medication (what he calls the "water wings" approach). He emphasizes that medication alone cannot retrain the brain; rather, it's a skill that has to be learned and practiced like any other. Dr. Schwartz outlines this training in four steps. Though the method was initially devised for OCD sufferers, the principles apply more generally to anxiety of all kinds.

Here is how you can apply it when you're overthinking.

Step 1: Relabel: Recognize that intrusive thoughts and urges are symptoms of overthinking, not personal flaws. They are also false alarms and not genuine signals of danger. When you label these thoughts as what they really are, they lose their power. For those with OCD, calling them obsessions and compulsions acknowledges their lack of grounding in reality. Overthinkers and worriers can do the same by correctly naming their thoughts as rumination and not genuinely helpful problem-solving. Your goal is to focus on controlling your responses to these thoughts rather than trying to eliminate the thoughts themselves, and certainly not to engage with them.

For example, you feel a little unwell and have a headache. The thought occurs to you that you are getting seriously ill and perhaps have a viral infection that will completely incapacitate you. You say to yourself, "Ah, I recognize this. I'm starting to ruminate. This is a false alarm."

Step 2: Reattribute: Understand that overthinking is a result of the overactivity of the brain's threat response. It's not comfortable or useful, but it's also not a major moral failing or evidence that you are broken or bad. Shift the perspective from personal responsibility to recognizing it as a symptom of overthinking. This symptom doesn't require your judgment and condemnation, but only your strategic intervention. Just breathe, observe what is happening, and take control.

Step 3: Refocus: Distraction gets a bad rap and rightly so when used to deny and avoid genuine issues. But if you already know that your rumination is just a misfiring of your threat alarm, you can safely ignore it and turn your attention elsewhere. Engage in activities like hobbies, walks, music, or exercise to divert attention from overthinking patterns. Be aware that arguing back against your rumination, judging it, dissecting it, and analyzing it are just more of the same. Just stop. There's no major willpower required; just switch your attention to a task that is healthy and meaningful to you. The urge to ruminate will pass quicker than you think.

Step 4: Revalue: Gradually reduce the significance placed on intrusive thoughts and urges, dismissing them more frequently. Cultivate the ability to distance yourself from overthinking by viewing it as a malfunctioning process, like a sticky manual transmission. While you work to question the ultimate value in overthinking, you may also ask yourself what else you can do with your mind, energy, and attention that would be more valuable to you. What are your goals and aspirations? What do you wish to contribute to the world? What is enjoyable? What is interesting? When you relax and open your attention, you can start to take these things in.

Summary:

- The solution to overthinking is not "underthinking" but the cultivation of *better thinking*.
- Creating psychological distance can separate us from our thoughts, feelings, and beliefs so we don't fuse with them or allow them to define us. This brings clarity.
- Freewriting or "brain dumping" involves unloading any thoughts, anxieties, to-do lists, and emotions onto paper to alleviate stress and free up mental space. Write freely and continually for twenty minutes and then look for repeating themes. You could also take a more structured

approach according to your needs and preferences.
- Anxiety mapping can help you distinguish between unhelpful rumination and helpful problem-solving, slow down, and get more organized. It can help you learn to better channel and train your thinking. Mind maps mirror the natural flow and structure of ideas in the human brain and offer a centralized, organized, and hierarchical representation of concepts, making them easier to comprehend, recall, and utilize. A good anxiety mind map can help you turn a rumination into a toll you can use to improve your life.
- Learn to turn off the "false alarms" of anxiety, which are driven by the brain's tendency to misjudge situations, misread others' intentions, and misinterpret internal sensations. This is a natural feature of the brain's threat response system, but we can override it.
- Try to adjust your perception and perspective. Stop and become aware of what is happening, and try to objectively re-evaluate the threat.
- Ask yourself: What is the perceived threat? How likely is it to happen? If it

did happen, how bad would it really be? How did you handle such a thing in the past, and how could you handle it again? Might *engaging* with the threat be worth it? To find calm again, "relabel, reattribute, refocus, and revalue."

Chapter 3: Get Grounded

Understanding your feelings and finding clarity in your thoughts will drastically reduce feelings of overwhelm—many people will find that these two steps alone can significantly curb their anxious overthinking. In this chapter, we'll consider another approach, which is to ground yourself back to reality.

Anxiety is a loose, vague, and fantastical thing of undetermined size and infinite proportions. But the real world right in front of us, however, is a lot smaller and easier to manage! Let's explore how to re-engage with the facts of our reality and deal with the practical issues that may be stressing us out.

Don't Take Your Own Word for It

Margaret suffers from anxiety and overthinking. She comes home from a casual get-together one day and starts ruminating. When her friends laughed, were they laughing with her or *at* her? Did she say something really stupid? Why did that person look at her that way and what did it mean? Were they all talking about her right now? She replays certain scenes over again and again in her mind like an awful video recording, pausing and replaying over the most uncomfortable parts. The whole thing makes her feel almost queasy with worry.

A few days later, a friend who went to the same get-together makes a random comment to Margaret, saying, "Well, you certainly made an impression the other night!" Margaret bursts into tears, all her worst fears confirmed. "What's wrong?" says the friend. "I was only going to say that a guy there asked me for your number. I think he's interested."

Anxiety can warp the way we interpret everything. In a very real way, Margaret created a whole new reality for herself, then stepped into it, assuming it was reality itself. Margaret's anxiety so distorted the way she processed information that she perceived neutral and even positive information as a threat. Rumination has a nasty habit of slowly disconnecting us from reality and inching us closer and closer to our own expectations, assumptions, and fears. That is, unless we make a conscious effort to question ourselves.

This process is called reality testing. If you're a media savvy person, you probably already know not to "believe everything you read." This is the same principle, except you are committing to not "believing everything you think."

Anxious people can get caught in a trap where they constantly engage with their *picture* of reality, and not reality itself. If anxiety becomes pronounced enough and goes on for long enough, life can start to feel really "off." You may feel lost, confused, foggy. During intense moments of anxiety, particularly during panic attacks, derealization may occur as a coping mechanism. This phenomenon involves the brain shutting down certain components to deal with overwhelming stress. As a result, people can feel totally disconnected from reality, experiencing sensations of unreality or unfamiliarity with their surroundings.

Anxiety-induced cognitive distortions further exacerbate the sense of distorted reality. These distortions can lead you to interpret and overthink situations in a negative or exaggerated manner, further hindering your ability to process information and maintain focus. Physical symptoms associated with anxiety, such as light-headedness or hyperventilation, can also affect sensory perception, making it difficult to perceive the external environment accurately.

As scary as all this sounds, the solution is simply to ground back in reality again. Thankfully, this is something anyone can achieve at any point, no matter how far into an anxiety loop they are. The idea is simply to reconnect to your five senses and the present moment. Try the 5-4-3-2-1 technique, where you try to look around the room and find five things you can see, four things you can touch, three things you can hear, two things you can smell, and one thing you can taste (or variations on this theme). This will instantly calm and ground you because it brings you back into the most important aspect of reality—the fact that it is only happening right *now*.

Reality Testing Your Thoughts

Once you're feeling calmer, it's possible to take a more skeptical stance on your own anxious thoughts. Reality testing is a fundamental concept in cognitive behavioral therapy (CBT) that helps people examine their thoughts and perceptions objectively by relying on concrete, objective data. In CBT, it's understood that thoughts, feelings, and behaviors are interconnected, and altering one aspect can influence the others. Since changing feelings directly can be challenging, reality testing focuses on modifying behaviors or thoughts to bring about positive changes.

In practical terms, reality testing involves scrutinizing one's thoughts and perceptions by evaluating evidence that supports or contradicts them.

Step 1: Identify the negative thought, belief, or assumption

First, is it a thought or a feeling? A prediction? A judgment or appraisal? Remind yourself that it is not reality that you are engaging with, but reality *as it appears through your set of filters*. So, look at the filters. Are they helping or hindering?

Are you applying an absolute rating to yourself, such as "I'm lazy," "I'm unlikable," or "I'm dumb"?

Are you jumping to conclusions ("I failed at this so I will fail at everything else") or mind reading ("She's probably angry at me; I can just tell")?

Are you overgeneralizing ("Everything sucks") or discounting the positive ("This award is only because they feel sorry for me")?

Just notice what you're thinking and feeling and put a label on it. Notice it *as* a thought and *as* a feeling, rather than just how things are.

Step 2: Gather some data

Now, look for evidence for and against the thoughts and beliefs you've identified.

One way to do this is to divide a sheet of paper into two sections. In the first column, write down the traits, behaviors, and thoughts of someone who fully embodies the negative label. For example, if the label is "lazy," describe someone who sleeps all day, mooches off others, etc. In the next column, write down your own actions and traits. Be as neutral and objective as possible—as though you were an impartial third party merely observing your life rather than passing judgment on it.

Another approach is to gather evidence for and against your thought. For example, if you put the thought "everything sucks" at the top of your page, fill the left-hand side with things you are unhappy about, but in the right-hand side, see if you can list evidence that everything does not suck (i.e., note down all the things that are going well for you, the things you're grateful for, your strengths and virtues, and even things that are just neutral).

The key to doing this exercise correctly is to clear your mind and approach the situation with genuine curiosity, almost as though you are a scientific investigator or a member of a jury in a court, hearing the evidence in a case. Try not to "fix the game" by actively working toward the conclusion you really want. To stay objective, it might help to imagine that you are doing this entire process for a friend or a stranger.

Step 3: Analyze your data

Now, take a look at the information you've gathered about this particular idea or event, and see if you can come to a sound, reasonable conclusion. If you're comparing the traits of an objectively lazy person with your own traits, how much overlap can you see? Factually and objectively speaking, are there differences? Are the lists one hundred percent the same? What stands out to you?

If you are gathering evidence for and against a belief, take a look and see how the lists compare. If, for example, the belief is "everything sucks," then is this really compatible with a sizeable list of things that do *not* suck?

Step 4: Have compassion

Looking at the data you have, how would you react if it belonged to someone you knew and loved, or to a stranger? Imagine that what you are seeing applies to a very young child, or indeed yourself when you were just a child. How do you feel about this information now?

Perhaps there is *some* evidence that you are behaving in a lazy way, or perhaps there are some things that are quite negative in your life right now. Even so, what attitude would you take to this information if it was a loved one experiencing it and not yourself? Would you be as critical of them as you are of yourself? Consider showing yourself the same compassion you would extend to others. Sometimes, a distorted thought is one that may be factually correct but is still unnecessarily mean. Choose instead to be nice to yourself!

Step 5: Gain clarity and identify areas for change

If you've worked through the first four steps, the fifth should come naturally. Through consciously asking yourself to find evidence for and against your beliefs and thoughts, you test them against reality and get a clearer and more realistic view. Is it really true that you're a lazy person? No. You adjust this a little; you may have some trouble right now dealing with a specific task, but that doesn't mean you are a lazy person. And even though some things are challenging, it doesn't mean that every single thing in your life is a problem.

Through this process, we can begin to realize that we are often our own worst enemies and that the source of much of our anxiety and discomfort in life is US! This can be a moment of revelation since it means that we can change, and therefore reduce the level of anxiety we experience.

In time, and with practice, you can learn to deploy the above process very quickly and even automatically. But in the beginning, take your time and move through the steps deliberately and carefully.

Finally, note that this process is not about reassurance. You are not trying to convince yourself that everything is just fine and that you have no reason to worry about anything. Even if you did try to placate yourself this way, you probably wouldn't believe it, right? Instead, the goal is to find a more moderate, realistic, and reasonable appraisal of yourself, others, and the situations you find yourself in. From that position, you can take purposeful action. There may indeed be a problem, but you will be able to see this problem so much more clearly and manage it so much more effectively if you are not adding your own harmful distortions.

Check the Facts

Imagine you've just taken an important exam, and on the way back home, you start to worry about how it went. You think about the few questions you found difficult and wonder if you should have answered them a little differently. Then you start thinking about how everyone else seemed to find the exam pretty easy. Do they know something you don't? You even start to have some pretty scary thoughts and wonder—did you even write the correct paper? Did you forget to put your name on it? Maybe at this very moment, a marker is looking at your paper and shaking their head at how awful your answers are and how badly you've failed...

The process goes a little like this:

Event → thoughts → emotions

Exam → "I've failed—I just know it" → panic and anxiety

Later, someone asks you, "What's up with you? You seem stressed." You reply by saying, "I'm anxious because of my exam!"

But actually, if you look at the sequence of events above, you are not in fact anxious because of the exam, but because of your *thoughts* about the exam. When we're caught up in anxiety, we can forget that we are having thoughts and feelings at all. That middle bit becomes invisible to us. It's that middle bit, however, where all the anxiety is actually coming from.

Dialectical behavior therapy (DBT) is a third-wave cognitive behavioral approach that focuses on emotional regulation skills. These techniques aim to interrupt thought spirals, provide structure to thoughts, and focus on what is within one's control. One technique you can use to reduce overthinking is to **check the facts**.

Checking the facts is a way to anchor us back into the reality of a situation and remind us that although our emotions are valid, they're not necessarily true, and they don't always provide the full picture. Again, recognizing this, we remember that emotions are "data, not directives."

In the above example, what are the facts? There aren't too many. You took an exam. It hasn't been marked yet. That's about it. Everything else is conjecture, prediction, speculation, interpretation, fear, and emotion.

Checking the facts is a particularly useful skill when we find ourselves catastrophizing or jumping to the worst possible conclusions based on limited information. It acknowledges that many emotions and actions stem from our interpretations of events rather than the events themselves (event → thoughts → emotions). Moreover, our emotions can heavily influence how we perceive events (event → emotions → thoughts).

By examining our thoughts and verifying the facts, we can:

- adjust our emotions or diminish their intensity
- or accept and acknowledge our emotions as they are, but refuse to let them control us
- or both!

Have Your Emotions; Don't Let Them Have You

Overthinking is not just cognitive. It's an *anxiety* disorder, and anxiety is an emotion. Try the following series of questions when you feel yourself getting carried away with anxiety or any other emotion.

Question 1: What's the emotion?

You should be familiar with this by now! The first step is always awareness and giving your experiences the right names and labels. What are you feeling? Note where that is in your body. What is the intensity of the sensation?

Example: I feel panicky. I can't relax. I'm on edge because I think something awful is coming—i.e., I'll find out soon that I've failed my exam.

Question 2: What prompted this feeling?

Now you're starting to put the pieces together. What came before? When exactly did you start to feel this way, and why? Sometimes we're quite mistaken about what really prompts or triggers an emotion. Here, we stick to the facts. No assumptions, no foregone conclusions, no guesswork. Just the facts.

Example: You think about it and realize that it's not the exam itself that triggered you into rumination, but rather a short conversation you had with a fellow student afterward. They casually mentioned finding question five easy, prompting you to remember that you actually found it tricky.

Question 3: How am I interpreting the prompting event?

This is the most important step. We need to identify that middle bit that contains all our assumptions and thoughts about a neutral event—i.e., the filter we're placing over the event. Simply asking this question can be illuminating because it alerts us to the fact that, yes, we are likely adding our own interpretations to things, often unconsciously and automatically.

Example: Your attention now drawn to question five, you realize you've generated a whole universe of negative interpretations and assumptions. Your answer was obviously wrong, and the other student's answer was obviously right. You're stupid and lazy and didn't study enough. Getting one question wrong means the whole paper is a failure. When you consider all these interpretations, you realize how few facts there are! You realize just how negative your filter on this event really is.

Question 4: Are there any alternative explanations?

You don't have to launch into an argument with yourself or go on a serious fact-finding mission. Just become curious if there may be another way to look at things that you haven't yet considered. Are there some facts, conclusions, options, or perspectives that you've overlooked?

Example: It occurs to you that it's possible the other student got the answer wrong, and you got it right. You don't try to argue for or against this hypothesis; you just note that it's a potential alternative explanation. Your first guess is just one possibility. You also note that you could have indeed gotten question five wrong, but all the other questions were right (why didn't you think of that before?).

Question 5: Am I assuming a threat?

Are you making catastrophic predictions? Once that alarm has been rung, it's tempting to get swept along and assume that it's alerting you to a real problem. But check that this is actually the case first. Is there a threat or have you just *assumed* there is a threat? Often, the fact is that we are simply dealing with an unknown. An unknown is not automatically a threat. Again, explore alternative possible outcomes other than the worst-case scenario.

Example: Thinking carefully and sticking to the facts, you realize that there is a potential outcome you didn't consider—you could earn a poor or mediocre pass in the exam without failing outright. Panic makes us see in black and white, but you start to consider some grey areas. Maybe doing badly on this exam is not the end of the world, but more like a mild disappointment or a frustrating setback.

Question 6: What is this worst-case scenario, anyway?

You might feel like there is a big catastrophe looming, but look at it clear-eyed. Remember that sometimes we make ourselves anxious because our thoughts and interpretations tell us that something is a threat. But we also make ourselves anxious when we convince ourselves that we lack any ability to cope. So, this question asks you to face this potential catastrophe and get curious about it. What tools and strengths do you have to cope with it? How have you solved a problem like this in the past? What can you do here to change things? Is it even possible to (gasp) accept the situation?

Example: You allow yourself to consider that failing is a possibility. You allow yourself to ask, "So what?" Even if the worst came to pass, what happens then? You allow your mind to go there. Well, you'd just get back on your feet and do better next time. You would wake up the next morning and get on with your life. It wouldn't be pleasant, but you wouldn't fail the year or the term, and you'd have time to get your grade back up if you worked hard for the next exam.

Question 7: Is my emotion in proportion to the facts?

Feelings are valid. You feel what you feel. Nevertheless, it's possible that your emotional reactions are not accurately reflecting the reality of a situation and are not appropriate in intensity. If you're overwhelmed and anxious, there's a good chance that you could dial your feelings back a bit and find more comfort in a more measured response.

Example: Once you've talked yourself through the facts and your thoughts and feelings about them, you can start to see if they are proportional. You realize that you could probably turn the sense of emergency way down. In fact, once you start looking at the facts, you already start to feel less panicked. You're able to tell yourself, "Stop. There's nothing you can do about it now. Whatever the outcome, you can deal with it when it comes, but it hasn't come yet. Let's go and do something else useful."

As Shakespeare's Hamlet says, "There is nothing either good or bad, but thinking makes it so." The updated version for overthinkers is: "There is nothing innately worrying or stressful in life, but thinking makes it so."

Is there a genuine threat? Think clearly, appraise well, and **take appropriate action**. If there isn't (and almost always there isn't), then turn your attention to the way that your interpretations are creating your experience, and adjust accordingly.

In neither case, however, is overthinking required. The answer to the question "How much worrying should I be doing?" is always "None."

Avoid Stress by Avoiding Overcommitment

One obvious but often overlooked way we can get more grounded and reconnected to reality is to think practically about our limits—specifically, our time and energy limits. If you're an overthinker, there is a chance that you're also an overcommitter. In other words, your stress is caused not by internal mental clutter and rumination, but rather by the fact that you've genuinely got too much on your plate.

Overcommitment refers to the habit of taking on more tasks, responsibilities, or commitments than you can realistically handle given the available time and resources. People overcommit for all sorts of reasons, including the desire to be helpful, a tendency to take on others' problems, unclear boundaries on what tasks to accept or reject, pressure from authority figures, or just plain old difficulty in saying "no."

When people consistently overcommit, they create their own overwhelm. This stress is not a result of a cognitive distortion, however—anyone would be stressed trying to do the impossible! Overcommitted people often worry about letting themselves or others down, and that's why they promise more than they can deliver. This then leads to more stress and more overthinking. Add in some guilt, self-criticism, and genuine procrastination and you have an awful recipe for anxiety and negativity.

Sometimes people can come to believe that the only thing standing in their way is their mindset. While mindset really *is* everything, there are unavoidable limits. None of us have more than twenty-four hours a day, none of us are immortal and endlessly energetic, and none of us can be in two places at one time.

Occasionally, someone may battle with *both* problems of procrastination and overcommitment. Janey, for example, often feels overwhelmed and intimidated at the start of any new project, and so she puts it off and procrastinates. Because she feels so bad about being "lazy," she ends up overcommitting as a kind of defense or compensation. She gives herself an extra-heavy to-do list the following day and raises her standards and ambitions even higher. This only makes her feel even more intimidated, however, and so she procrastinates when it's time to act, and the cycle repeats. This is all to say that overcommitting doesn't mean you are necessarily super productive.

Overcommitment, like perfectionism, is a vice parading as a virtue. If you recognize some of this in yourself, then know that the way forward is not to beat yourself up for not being more motivated or having enough energy to do it all. It's not to sleep less or chastise yourself for not being organized. Rather, the solution is to consciously acknowledge and accept your limits and work within them.

Grounding is about facing the facts of your life as they are, and one way to respect your own limits is to proactively know your time budget. Of course, you have other resources—energy, for example—but time is arguably the most important one.

The time investment formula offers a mathematical framework to comprehend the connection between your expectations and actual time allocation. Being a formula, it helps you objectively quantify where you are spending your time and see in black and white whether things are adding up or are wildly out of balance. The great thing about a tool like the overcommitment formula is that it takes emotion out of the equation and quickly helps you bring clarity to the real ins and outs of your daily life.

By using this formula, you can assess your time budget objectively and identify any adjustments you can make to achieve a balanced schedule and reduce unnecessary stress.

The formula for time investment success is:

(External expectations) + (Internal expectations) ≤ 24 hours – (Self-care)

In words, that means that the total time spent on life's expectations and demands on you is less than or equal to the twenty-four hours you have in the day. The important bit, however, is that you also factor in self-care from those twenty-four hours.

If your formula is more like:

(External expectations) + (Internal expectations) > 24 hours – (Self-care)

. . . then you can expect "time debt stress," which is simply a way of naming the anxiety that comes from overcommitment. The above formula is actually a mathematical impossibility (talk about stressful!). The only fixed value in the formula is the twenty-four hours, which means that if our balance isn't looking great, we have only two options: adjust how much time we spend on our self-care or adjust our expectations.

How to Use the Overcommitment Formula

Step 1: Calculate your self-care number by identifying self-care categories and

calculate the hours you spend per category:

Break down your daily activities into three main categories. For example:

- Sleeping—8 hours
- Eating—1 hour
- Personal Grooming—1 hour

The term "self-care" here can be a bit misleading since it's not necessarily a focus on just yourself. Your self-care hours are, essentially, your life. No two people will be the same, and some activities will include both self-care and care for others. Some people need more or less sleep, and some may include things like sports, exercise, community work, and caring for their families as "self-care."

Play around with your own numbers until you find something you feel best represents your life. Add up the time values for each category to find your approximate self-care number:

Self-care number = Sleep + Eating + Personal grooming

The total is 10 hours.

Step 2: Assess your total commitments

Now to the left side of the formula. These are all the things that make claims on your time, whether these expectations come from other people or are generated by you yourself. List and categorize your external expectations (e.g., work, commute, pets, relationships) and internal expectations (e.g., hobbies, side projects, personal time).

If you are having trouble distinguishing between self-care and an internal expectation, ask yourself whether the activity is vital for sustaining your well-being, or if it's more aspirational, ambitious, recreational, or exploratory. Exercising thirty minutes a day may be *essential* for your health and well-being, whereas a special hike in beautiful natural surroundings is more of a treat or a pleasurable pastime. Of course, there is overlap and ambiguity; just make a judgment call based on what is a "must have" and what is a "nice to have" and go from there. When you're done, calculate the total hours.

For example:

- External expectations:
    - 8 for work + 1 for house and pet duties = 9 hours
- Internal expectations:
    - 2 for games and TV + 1 for reading + 1 for side projects = 4 hours

The total is 13 hours.

Step 3: Use the equation and substitute its values

Now plug your figures into your equation. To continue with our example:

(External expectations) + (Internal expectations) ≤ 24 hours – (Self-care)

(8 for work + 1 for house and pet duties) + (2 for games and TV + 1 for reading + 1 for side projects) ≤ 24 hours – (8 for sleep + 1 for eating + 1 for personal grooming)

(9) + (4) ≤ 24 hours – (10)

(13) ≤ (14)

Step 4: Evaluate the result

After adding up both sides, see what you think of the final equation. Is anything surprising or unexpected? What immediately jumps out at you?

Analyze your result. If the left side exceeds the right, it might mean that you are overcommitted and risking burnout. The greater the difference, the more extreme the overcommitment and associated stress. Look carefully at your figures, though, as this imbalance may also represent a misunderstanding about how you *really* spend your time every day. It may be worth taking a week to observe and record where your time is really going.

If the right side exceeds the left, then this is usually a good result and indicates that you are not routinely overextending yourself. Naturally, a right-hand side value that is very much higher than the left could indicate that you have an *under*-commitment problem, or that you are not making full use of your potential, time, or resources. Coud you be stuck in a rut? Might you need a little more challenge?

Step 5: Take inspired action

Sometimes when people feel overwhelmed and like their life is spiraling out of control, they try to do something to fix it. But the thing they try to do just becomes one more task on an already full to-do list. So, they end up trying to fix overcommitment by . . . committing some more!

Step 5 is about inspired action, but in this case, "action" may not mean one more task, but choosing *not* to do something, or else choosing to switch certain tasks with others. You'll have to be honest about your personal limits, goals, and values in order to identify what will work best for you. There are a few things you can do, however, if the above exercise reveals a habit of overcommitment:

- Do a "commitment audit" once a month to tally up everything that is currently making demands on your time or attention. See what you can renegotiate, delegate, ignore, or shuffle around.
- If there are repeated actions, see if you can automate them—for example, by creating an email template instead of writing similar emails over and over again.
- Pick the low-hanging fruit first. There may be many changes you need to make, but start with the easiest and most obvious one first. Just make one small change and try it for a week, then appraise and go from there.
- Check in with your goals and values. It's always useful to consider all the balls you're juggling, but don't forget to regularly tune in with all those things that are most important to you. Are you carving out enough non-negotiable time for them?
- Finally, just say no. If you identify a boundary that needs firming up, politely and assertively say no, knowing that this doesn't mean you are

lazy or unkind or unambitious—it just means you cannot magically make the day longer than twenty-four hours!

Summary:

- We can reduce anxiety by checking the facts and grounding back in reality. One way to do this is by grounding in the five senses, which are always connected to the present moment.
- Reality testing is a concept in cognitive behavioral therapy (CBT) that helps people examine their thoughts and perceptions objectively by relying on concrete, objective data. First, identify the negative thoughts, beliefs, or assumptions and then gather and analyze some data for and against them. Using plenty of self-compassion and non-judgment, you can then gain a clearer and more realistic view of the situation and identify areas for change, if any.
- Remind yourself that it is not reality that you are engaging with, but reality *as it appears through your set of filters*. Be mindful of cognitive distortions, and stay neutral, curious, and kind.
- The goal is to find a more moderate, realistic, and reasonable appraisal of

the situation, and from there, take purposeful action. "Check the facts" is a way to anchor back into reality and remember that although our emotions are valid, they're not necessarily true, and they don't always provide the full picture.
- Many emotions and actions stem from our interpretations of events rather than the events themselves. Identify what you're feeling, identify your interpretations of events, and identify possible alternatives. Check that you're not making assumptions and confusing a feeling with reality.
- An unknown is not automatically a threat. Is there a genuine threat? Think clearly, appraise well, and take appropriate action. If not, get curious about your interpretations.
- Finally, be realistic about your boundaries and limits and think carefully about how you use time. Overcommitment can sometimes exacerbate overthinking.

Chapter 4: Gather Yourself

In Chapter 1 we explored ways to begin taking responsibility and ownership of your own feelings and acknowledging and accepting them for what they are—real. Becoming adept at using your emotions as data, and understanding especially how anxiety works, we become masterful at managing our own experience.

In Chapter 2 we took a closer look at the content of our beliefs and thought patterns and tried to uncover healthy, useful thinking even though it may sometimes be hiding in a tangle of rumination and worry.

And in Chapter 3 we took a practical and realistic look at one surefire way to tackle anxiety: grounding ourselves in reality. By being realistic about the facts and about our own limits, we teach ourselves to get out of our heads and reconnect with the real world.

In this chapter we're going even deeper and exploring what is arguably **your most powerful personal resource: your attention**. Your conscious awareness in the moment is, in many ways, all you have. For us overthinkers, the present moment is continually passed over while our attention gets yanked to the past, the future, or some hypothetical no-man's-land that simply isn't real. If catastrophizing, worrying, and panic are a problem for you, then your attention and awareness may be fractured, widely dispersed, or chaotic. In this chapter, we're looking at how to *gather ourselves* and bring all the threads of our conscious awareness back to the center, which we learn to hold with calm control.

The Observing Mind: Watch Thoughts . . . and Let Them Go

In many Buddhist traditions and mindfulness-based approaches like acceptance-commitment therapy (ACT), there are two types of mind: the "Thinking Mind" and the "Observing Mind." We can only be in one or the other—never both at the same time.

The Thinking Mind is characterized by constant chatter, self-talk, interpretations, judgments, guesses, impulsive reactions, and arguments. Most often, this internal chatter is just noise and clutter, but for those of us with anxiety issues or the habit of overthinking, this constant mental churning can create emotional distress. As we've seen in previous chapters, our thoughts act like a filter between us and reality, telling us what reality means and so prompting certain emotional reactions. This filter is a product of the Thinking Mind, which is capable of generating infinite thoughts, theories, stories, and beliefs.

The Observing Mind, on the other hand, simply watches without judgment or engagement.

It refers to a state of mindfulness where people are able to observe their thoughts without getting caught up or entangled in them. It involves cultivating an awareness of one's thoughts, emotions, and sensations without judgment or attachment. Instead of trying to suppress or control thoughts, people in an observer mind state practice acceptance and non-reactivity to whatever arises in their internal experience.

It's important to understand what is meant here by "attachment." One day you may be meditating and think to yourself, "Wow, look how calm and Zen I'm being. I'm so good at meditation!" This might make you feel a warm sense of pride and superiority. This "positive" feeling, however, is just as much part of the Thinking Mind as a thought like, "You're so stressed. Look at how bad you are at meditation!" The idea is to neither cling nor avoid. Both are a form of attachment. Instead, we pull back and simply become aware. No interpretation, no value judgment either way.

The trick lies in acknowledging *all* of your experiences as temporary and transient, rather than identifying with them. The idea is to see that these experiences are just part of a flow, just emergent events, and not your true essence. We are practicing the art of taking psychological distance to its limits.

Rather than fusing with a temporary experience ("I'm bad at meditation"), we can step back and see that we are simply having a thought right now about being bad at meditation. Again, we are not trying to push away the experience of feeling bad (that's just more attachment and engagement), but neither are we holding on to it tightly. All we do is sit still, in the moment, and notice what is happening. This is awareness.

The meditation habit can understandably take a lifetime to master, but it really is very simple. The more we can teach ourselves to constantly re-gather our awareness and to avoid needlessly attaching and engaging, the more we are able to see that so much of what our Thinking Mind throws at us is, well, nonsense. Just noise. It's there one moment and gone the next. How much of what flies around our mind is "real," anyway? When you go still within yourself, you start to notice that the answer may be "Not much." This brings a sense of calm control that goes far deeper than ordinary stress management or relaxation. You find peace and serenity in parallel with your constantly changing experience.

How to Cultivate Your Observing Mind

Exercise 1: Disidentification with thoughts and emotions

When experiencing strong emotions or thoughts, disidentify with them by expressing them as temporary states rather than permanent conditions. Much of your perception in this area is shaped by the language you use and the way you speak about your experiences. The way we speak can make us believe that our temporary experiences are permanent, pervasive, and personal—i.e., they will last forever, they apply to everything and everyone everywhere, and they are especially connected to us as people in a way that defines us. But we can change our language to reflect the fact that almost all experiences are temporary, limited, and impersonal—i.e., things aren't always happening TO US, but rather just happening.

For example, you could say, "I'm a depressive," or, "I'm depressed," and this implies that the temporary feeling of depression is actually a permanent fact of life and even part of your identity. If you say, however, "I'm noticing some depressing thoughts right now," then suddenly you scale the experience down to size. It's no longer so big that it expands to fill everything; it's simply something that is happening. We can go into Observing Mind and just become aware.

Exercise 2: Thanking your Thinking Mind

One potential trap is to get into a "gotcha!" mentality, where you go on the hunt for attachment in yourself and pounce on it when you find it. You may end up inadvertently self-criticizing and more self-conscious than self-aware.

A way around this is to simply express a little compassion and gratitude toward negative thoughts and emotions—this is a technique borrowed more from acceptance and commitment therapy (ACT) than Zen meditation. Remember that your Thinking Mind is not some horrible demon that's out to get you, and it's not a flaw or a moral failing to have a Thinking Mind in the first place. In fact, this function of your mind is just a tool, and in the past, it has probably helped you in countless ways to make sense of your world, to cope, and even to thrive.

Mindfulness is not a "no pain, go gain" activity! Instead of thinking, "What an idiot. There you go again with all the same old chatter . . ." think, "Thank you, Thinking Mind, for feeling nervous before my date tonight. I can tell you're trying to help." Immediately, you can let some of that nervousness go. Remember that you don't ever have to argue with thoughts or chastise yourself for having them or try to coax or convince yourself into having a better attitude. The great thing about the Observing Mind is how relaxing it is—you don't have to *do* anything. Just be there. When you can pull back this way, you realize that the thoughts and emotions actually have no power—it was only your attention and belief that was giving them that power.

Exercise 3: Cut big scary thoughts down to size

Are you a catastrophizer? Are you someone who can't help dwelling for ages on the worst-case scenario? When feeling overwhelmed by a particular thought or emotion, we may not realize how *serious* we're making things. Without realizing it, we take a fairly neutral situation and make it feel high stakes and ultra-important. But is it really? One technique of dialing back the intensity is to deliberately view your thoughts with less seriousness. Deliberately make them silly or absurd. Visualize a cartoon character saying the thoughts in a ridiculous voice, or picture the doom scenario playing out like a comic scene complete with a laugh track of clownish sound effects.

Exercise 4: Watch your thoughts on a screen

When you are watching a movie on a screen, you may get deeply caught up in the storyline and the emotions the characters are portraying... but in the back of your mind, you always know that none of it's really "true," and that at any moment you could easily remember that you're still sitting there in the theater, popcorn in your lap.

You can do the same thing with the "movies" that you show yourself in your own mind. Many of us are trapped in endless reruns of the same old blockbusters—and many of them are painful dramas, horrors, or nail-biting thrillers. When you zoom out and imagine that you're watching your experience on a screen just the same as you'd watch a movie, you remind yourself that you have the choice when it comes to how engrossed you want to become. In fact, you could even get up and walk out of the movie theater!

Imagine a blank screen and practice projecting thoughts, memories, and mental images onto it. Be the audience, not one of the actors inside the screen. As thoughts appear on your screen, just watch them come and go, remaining curious about the thinking and observing process without judgment. Sometimes thoughts may dominate the screen and capture your attention, while other times there will be something boring and uneventful happening, or it may be blank. Just keep noticing and watching. How does being the audience to your own thoughts change the way you feel about them?

Give Your Attention a Workout

How successful were you with the exercises suggested in the previous section? Chances are you could manage to stay mindful and disengaged for a while . . . but eventually something popped up to distract you, right? Maybe you "came to" and suddenly realized that you had followed a trail of thought and were completely engrossed in it for a few minutes, before remembering the original task you were meant to be focusing on.

How is overthinking connected to attention? When you overthink, every "false alarm" and distraction burst into your field of awareness and completely command your attention. Then, another thing bursts in a few seconds later, and you follow that. And so on and so on. It's as if your mind is wild and runs rampant and cannot be held in any one place. We can blame social media and an information-dense modern world to some extent, but the truth is that our ability to focus is not free—it's a skill we have to purposely develop.

It would be silly to get discouraged or impatient if you find it difficult to train and focus your attention. Instead, commit to practicing just the same as you would exercise a muscle. The attention training technique (ATT) is a component of metacognitive therapy (MCT) and is designed to empower people to control their attention effectively. The primary goal of ATT is to disrupt harmful thinking patterns such as worry and rumination by strengthening metacognitive beliefs. The big idea is that you have the capacity to redirect your attention away from distressing thoughts and toward the present moment. That capacity may be a little weak and undeveloped . . . but you have it!

Mindfulness-based attention training can be thought of as a workout for your attention. If you're a skilled ruminator, you probably have had years and years of practice letting fear command and control you. The ATT approach is about doing the opposite and strengthening your *choice* in where you want your attention to go. Mindfulness entails observing the present moment with acceptance, and that means accepting it all, whether it's sensations, thoughts, or feelings. By noticing distractions and continually redirecting attention to the present moment, your will and awareness grows stronger.

Mundane Task Focusing

During mundane household chores like washing dishes or ironing, our minds often wander on autopilot. That's only natural. However, these moments actually provide ideal opportunities to practice channeling our attention. Mundane task focusing involves deliberately sustaining attention on such activities, effectively exercising our attention "muscle." The advantage of this practice is that it doesn't require additional time in our day (hooray for the time budget!). Rather, it involves a simple shift in *how* we attend to tasks we already perform.

STEPS:

1. Take a moment to think about the various everyday routine tasks you do that you could use to exercise your attention (e.g., doing the dishes, hanging washing, gardening, taking a shower, vacuuming, eating a meal, brushing your teeth, walking, etc.).
2. Pick one of these tasks for your first attention workout and record when and where you will do it on the "Attention Workout Worksheet" (see below).
3. Now, start the task without intentionally trying to work your attention. You may wish to gauge your "pre-workout" attention levels by rating the percentage of your attention that is currently focused on yourself (including on your own thoughts, bothersome symptoms and sensations, feelings, etc.) versus the percentage currently focused on the task at hand.

4. Now, whilst doing the task, you can officially start your attention workout. Each time you notice your mind has wandered off the task, anchor your attention back to the task by focusing, non-judgmentally, on the following:

• Touch: What does the activity feel like? What is the texture like (e.g., rough, smooth)? Where on your body do you have contact with this task? Are there areas of your body with more or less contact?

• Sight: What do you notice about the task? What catches your eye? How does the task appear? What about the light, the shadows, the contours, the colors?

• Hearing: What sounds do you notice? What kinds of noises are associated with the task? How are these sounds connected to the other sense information you're receiving?

• Smell: What smells do you notice? Do they change during the task? How many smells are there? What are they really *like*, these smells?

• Taste: What flavors do you notice? Do they change during the task? What is the quality of the flavors? Can you play around with the distinction between smell, touch, and taste? Can you see exactly where those boundaries might be?

Of course, you don't actually have to write down the answers to these questions. Simply use them to help you become aware of all the sensory aspects of the task (i.e., touch, sight, hearing, smell, taste) that you could focus on during your attention workout. Let these sensations dominate your awareness and anchor your attention back to the task at hand.

5. Once you have completed the mundane task-focusing activity, you may wish to re-rate how much of your attention was self versus task focused, and think about what you have learned from completing the activity. Be careful, however, and avoid doing the activity while thinking about how you plan to complete the worksheet when you're done!

With repeated practice, you may start to notice that you actually enjoy being so deeply and fully absorbed in an activity. Paradoxically, such close and full attention can be profoundly relaxing and can create powerful feelings of timelessness, depth, and ease. Many people find the concept of sitting meditation a strange one. It can seem like a big ask to schedule a discrete period of time in your day where you're just meditating—it's a lot of pressure! Mundane task focusing, however, incorporates mindfulness into your real, everyday life. The plain ordinariness of this exercise is what makes it so effective.

As you practice more of this kind of exercise, keep reminding yourself that you are in control of your attention. It doesn't matter what your emotional state is or what is happening around you. You decide where you place your focus. The more you cultivate this skill, the easier it will be for you to gain some useful distance from intrusive or unhelpful thoughts that pop up and invite you to start a rumination loop.

In time, you may gather fresh evidence that counters previously held beliefs and assumptions about yourself, such as "I can't stop ruminating" or "My overthinking controls me" or "I have no say over where my attention goes."

It's now known that people with mood and attention disorders tend to have an extreme self-focus and may endlessly monitor their own internal states. The goal is not to do more inward reflection, but to turn outward and to train the attention to stay on the target that you choose. While doing a mundane task, you may notice your mind continually inviting you inward to mull over some thought or other. You have to continually bring it back outside of yourself and back onto the external task.

One final caveat: your goal is not perfection. When you go to the gym to lift weights, your goal is not to lift that bar so perfectly that it stays lifted forever. Rather, the point of exercise is the continual effort that is being made. In the same way, the goal of attention training is not to have pure one hundred percent focus on the task or a perfectly blank mind (although if you can achieve this once in a while, that's great!). The goal is to keep practicing the effort of pulling your attention back to where you want it. This means that you don't need to get frustrated or discouraged if you notice your attention wandering. Just imagine that every time you gently pull it back, it's like doing a "rep" in the attention gym, and you've just strengthened yourself a tiny bit more. That's something to celebrate!

My Attention Workout

Mundane task: _____
Where and when will I do my workout: _____

Before starting the attention workout, where do I notice my attention is focussed?

- Self-focussed attention (i.e., focussing on thoughts, feelings, symptoms, etc): _____ %
- Task-focussed attention (i.e., the task I was actually engaged with): _____ %

100 %

During the attention workout, anchor my attention back to the task at hand by focussing on:

- <u>Touch</u>: What does the activity feel like? What is the texture like (e.g., rough, smooth)? Where on my body do I have contact with the task? Are there areas of my body with more or less contact with the task?
- <u>Sight</u>: What do I notice about the task? What catches my eye? How does the task appear? What about the light... the shadows... the contours... the colours?
- <u>Hearing</u>: What sounds do I notice? What kinds of noises are associated with the task?
- <u>Smell</u>: What smells do I notice? Do they change during the task? How many smells are there?
- <u>Taste</u>: What flavours do I notice? Do they change during the task? What is the quality of the flavours?

Remember that it is normal for my mind to wander off. Rather than beating myself up over this, use each time my mind wanders as an opportunity to workout my attention muscle again.

Having completed the attention workout, where did I notice my attention was focussed during the workout?

- Self-focussed attention (i.e., focussing on thoughts, feelings, symptoms, etc): _____ %
- Task-focussed attention (i.e., the task I was actually engaged with): _____ %

100 %

What did I learn from this? What conclusions can I make from this?

_____
_____

The aim is to complete this worksheet the first time you try your mundane task focusing so you have a bit of guidance about what to do with your attention. You don't need to complete it every time you do a mundane task focusing exercise.

The Worst Case, the Best Case, and the Most Likely Case

Here's an interesting exercise you can try for yourself right now. Cast your mind back to a situation in your past that you were anxious about. At the time, perhaps you were terrified about how it might have turned out and imagined the worst.

But what *did* end up happening? If you think about it now, chances are the outcome you feared never really came. Even if you did experience some adversity or difficulty, you probably found that it wasn't quite so bad as you thought, and you were a lot better equipped to deal with it than you imagined. Today, you may barely give this event a second thought.

When people catastrophize, they tend to magnify the severity of potential outcomes and actively conjure up worst-case scenarios. They scare themselves to death, in other words. Catastrophizers often blow small problems out of proportion, choosing the worst aspect to focus on and then amplifying this to its worst possibility and acting as though that thing is already, in some way, true. It's a little like self-hypnosis, where they convince themselves that even minor setbacks will lead to totally disastrous consequences.

When the event doesn't actually come to pass in that way, we sometimes fail to notice and retroactively adjust our assumptions when we realize our predictions were wrong. Why? Maybe because we're already too busy worrying about the next thing!

This tendency is influenced and mediated by the brain's amygdala, which constantly assesses incoming stimuli for potential threats. The amygdala, however, is also heavily involved in the processing of emotions. You can think of the amygdala as a kind of storyteller. It takes all the incoming data it receives from the present moment and arranges it into a bigger picture. Most of us are not doing this in a neutral way, however, but are actually constructing narratives based on the narratives we constructed before—and the meaning and value we give to these stories are inextricably tied up to our emotions.

Past traumatic events can influence and distort our ability to accurately appraise what is happening right now. In other words, if we expect and anticipate a threat, our amygdala tends to arrange incoming stimuli to create a picture that justifies that emotional reality—it creates a picture that looks like a catastrophe.

Jay Stringer, a mental health professional, suggests that understanding unresolved traumas is more effective than simply trying to suppress catastrophizing tendencies. Catastrophizing is something we do as a symptom of an overactive threat-appraisal, and this is often a kind of learned behavior. We may have fallen into the habit of defaulting to an exaggerated, negative mentality that automatically anticipates painful experiences, simply because at some point, that behavior was reinforced in us. Perhaps tragedy really did strike and we felt unable to cope, or perhaps we were raised by parents who taught us, one way or another, that disaster was always just around the corner. Catastrophizing, then, is a cognitive error that manifests as magnification and distortion. But it has an emotional root and often stems from feelings of helplessness, uncertainty, and fear.

If catastrophizing is learned behavior, then it stands to reason that it can be unlearned. It requires that we actually test our assumptions that the worst thing can and will happen, and that we won't be able to cope when it does. Because anxiety narrows and distorts our awareness so much, it often quietly works to shift our attention away from evidence that would go against our worst fears. We just quickly rearrange the incoming data again so that we are still telling the same narrative of disaster.

The "worst case, best case, and most likely case" technique involves actively considering various potential outcomes of a situation. It's a way to force yourself to consider information that you might be automatically and unconsciously ignoring out of habit. It encourages people to think beyond solely the worst-case scenario, which they may often dwell on, and also contemplate the best-case scenario and the most likely outcome. This can be a useful way to ground and gather yourself.

Giving equal attention to *all* possibilities helps to balance perspectives and limit how far you can carry any particular idea. It helps you avoid getting stuck in negative thinking patterns or getting too preoccupied with information that looks the scariest and least tolerable. While planning for worst-case scenarios can be beneficial for preparedness, acknowledging and planning for best-case scenarios and the most likely outcomes is also valuable for a more well-rounded approach to decision-making and problem-solving. We can sometimes forget that, while there is a cost to ignoring a warning sign and preparing for a setback, there is also a cost to failing to recognize a good opportunity when it arises, or failing to properly enjoy and be grateful for what is currently working for you.

The Boring Truth

The boring truth is that the most likely outcome is one that is probably neither extremely good nor extremely bad. In all probability, the most likely thing to happen is something that falls somewhere in the middle. Looking back to your own history and all the ups and downs you've already been through, you might come to the same conclusion: *The very worst thing that could possibly happen* usually didn't, right?

That said, the skill we want to develop is not the skill of automatically dismissing any scary predictions about the future. Things don't always go to plan, and it's useful to acknowledge potential pitfalls so that you can prepare for them. A point to remember is that catastrophizing in itself is not useful anyway. Dwelling on possible catastrophes is *not* the same as being prepared . . . in fact it can often interfere with our ability to think clearly and strategically about the future. How do we learn a more balanced approach?

Try the following:

First, Identify Your Thoughts and Emotions

Begin by recognizing your thoughts and emotions surrounding the situation. Acknowledge any worries or fears you may have. Practice the all-important (non-judgmental) labeling. For example, you have a cello recital coming up and you're stressed about how it's going to go.

Next, Explore the Worst-Case Scenario

You don't have to forcefully restrain yourself. The anxious mind will push you to consider all the most threatening and extreme-sounding possibilities first, so let it. But do it consciously. If you like, you can even exaggerate the worst possible outcome—to comic proportions if you want to. Imagine the most extreme, negative consequences that could occur.

In our example, let's say the worst-case scenario is that it's a total flop. Your teacher is clearly embarrassed, you ruin the whole performance for all the other musicians, and you sneeze mid-performance, breaking your bow. The performance is so bad that it has to be stopped, people in the audience start booing, and a small child in the front row bursts into tears. Then, you literally die of shame, right there on the stage (an exaggeration, but close to how you feel!).

Explore the Best-Case Scenario

Now that you've got that out of your system, spend a little time imagining the best possible outcome. Isn't it funny how seldom we actually do this? Envision the most favorable, positive consequences that could occur. How could things turn out even better than you imagined? Dream big and visualize scenarios where everything goes exceptionally well.

For example, you play perfectly and not only do you give an excellent performance, but you also have a really enjoyable time, and several people compliment and praise you after the show. Maybe you win a prestigious prize and later discover that a headhunter had been sitting secretly in the audience and, based on your incredible performance, wants to hire you immediately for your dream job.

Explore the Most Likely Scenario

Now that you've identified the very upper and lower limits of what the outcome might be, try to take a more realistic view of where you're most likely to fall in between. Consider the circumstances and your understanding of the *facts* of the situation and find a probable middle ground. In our example, this may look like feeling nervous and making a few small mistakes at the start of the performance, but getting through it okay and finding that, for the most part, feedback is encouraging and positive. You may even decide to explore a few different possibilities here, across a range, some a little more negative/positive than others. Just keep them realistic and based on the facts.

Reflect on the Three Scenarios You've Envisioned

Take a look at all the possibilities. How does it feel to take them all in, compared to only dwelling on the worst case? Looking at them again and considering how likely each one really is, where would you like to place your focus and attention? Do you still feel anxious? More importantly, do you still *want* to feel anxious, given that the very worst is likely to not happen?

It may be useful to consciously acknowledge the consequences of your overthinking. What does it cost you to ruminate this way? Think of all the things you lose by not being calmer and more relaxed about the future. What does your overthinking and catastrophizing prevent you from doing and achieving?

One of the real tragedies to catastrophizing is how it wastes our time, energy, and attention. Is there a better place to invest this time, energy, and attention so that it might actually bring you rewards? In our example, given the most likely outcome, what is the best investment of your attention and resources?

Let's say that after this deliberation, you decide that rather than stress about what might happen, it's wiser to just take action and be as prepared as you can. You commit to practicing a little more before the rehearsal, knowing that you can relax more in the certainty that you've done what you can. Nothing is more calming than making a conscious effort to improve the real facts of your present situation!

Summary:

- Your most powerful personal resource is your attention, but for overthinkers, our attention is often fractured, chaotic, dispersed, or wildly out of our control. The present moment is continually passed over while our attention gets yanked to the past, the future, or unreal hypotheticals. Being in the Observing Mind rather than the Thinking Mind helps us cultivate non-attachment and pure awareness. Understanding the transient and unreal nature of our thoughts, we do not attach to them.
- Almost all experiences are temporary, limited, and impersonal, and things aren't always happening TO US, but

rather just happening. Remember that you don't have to argue with thoughts, chastise yourself for having them, or convince yourself to have a better attitude. You can even thank your Thinking Mind for trying to help, make fun of it, or watch it from afar as though it were just a movie you were seeing.
- Our ability to focus is a skill we have to purposely develop, and we can do so with mundane task focusing. This involves deliberately sustaining attention on trivial daily activities, effectively exercising our attention "muscle." Even if it's a little undeveloped, you have the capacity to redirect your attention away from distressing thoughts and outward, toward the present moment. You are in control. It doesn't matter what your emotional state is—you decide where you place your focus.
- Carefully distinguish between the worst-case scenario, the best-case scenario, and the most likely scenario. When people catastrophize, they magnify the severity of potential outcomes and actively conjure up worst-case scenarios. Catastrophizing is a cognitive error that manifests as magnification and distortion, often

stemming from past trauma. We need to deliberately widen our awareness and neutrally appraise threats in new ways. The boring truth is that the most likely outcome is one that is probably neither extremely good nor extremely bad.

Chapter 5: Be Still

For some people, stress is like water off a duck's back. What exactly is it about such people that allows them to remain so calm, at ease, and relaxed, whatever shape life takes around them? In this chapter, we're looking at what it means to not just temporarily overcome stress and anxiety, but to live a life of peace, poise, and purpose, whatever happens.

After years in therapy, Tara had a major insight: She realized that all the people she admired actually did not have lives any easier than hers. She finally understood that these people did not have simple, perfect, eternally comfortable lives—far from it! Rather, what was clear was that they had a very particular way of responding to their lives, which were filled with all the same obstacles, stresses, annoyances, and unknowns that she found in her own life.

Like many people, Tara had been unconsciously waiting for her life to finally be fixed and resolved once and for all. She is a perfectionist and had never stopped striving for some ideal end state when her life would be smooth and correct and she would no longer have to worry about anything.

The big epiphany hit her one day: Her life would never be perfect. She would have to find a way to relax and be at ease with her life *just as it was*. Right now. All at once, she looked at her idols with a new perspective and became curious not about how they managed to be perfect, but how they managed to be happy despite not being perfect. She realized that they didn't have everything under control but had learned to take conscious action and be content anyway. Tara now believes that this is in fact an underappreciated life skill: the courage to be calm and well in the midst of a life that is forever incomplete, imperfect, and uncertain.

Wabi-Sabi: Mindful Imperfectionism

Perfectionism is all about holding impossibly high standards. It naturally implies a degree of failure, because if your standards are high enough, then it's actually impossible to reach them—i.e., simply holding that standard means you *will* fail to meet them.

Thus, perfectionists are often also procrastinators. If you have a lofty standard to reach and know you cannot possibly reach it, it's obvious that you would avoid ever starting. For the worst perfectionists among us, they may talk themselves into a state of paralysis—from within this mindset, it is logically consistent to never **do** anything, but merely to continue to **have** high standards. You could end up with a well-developed and highly principled hypothetical life . . . but your real life never quite gets off the ground!

Individuals holding perfectionistic tendencies often experience chronic pressure to achieve flawlessness, leading to constant anxiety and negative self-talk. Even when they do achieve, they automatically discount it and never celebrate their accomplishments—they always could have done more. The fear of making mistakes, coupled with a lack of resilience in the face of adversity, only results in heightened stress levels . . . which ironically makes you far less effective and far less likely to do your best.

As you can guess, overthinking plays an important role in this cycle. The expectation of perfection is often a demand we place on ourselves, and our mind becomes a kind of slavedriver, constantly comparing what we are to what we "should" be. Is this enough? Am I enough? What will other people think? What if this all goes badly?

The physical toll of all this chronic pressure can manifest as headaches, muscle tension, and a host of other health issues. Perfectionism can strain relationships, often because we get into the habit of not engaging with people as they are, but with our own tangled mess of unrealistic expectations of who they *should* be. Faulty assumptions, hurtful comparisons, and misunderstandings may all branch off from the root of perfectionism.

How do you get better? Contrary to what many perfectionists fear, the way out is *not* to go to the other extreme and become lax, lazy, and mediocre! Managing perfectionism-related stress involves recognizing your tendencies and choosing to challenge them with compassion rather than more rules, demands, and expectations. Simply, the way out is to embrace imperfection.

Wabi-sabi is a Japanese concept embodying simplicity, humility, and the graceful acceptance of imperfection, particularly given the passage of time. The term originates from two words: "wabi," representing simplicity, humility, and natural living, and "sabi," signifying the beauty found in the process of aging or withering. Together, they convey something of the Buddhist understanding of impermanence, and the ideal attitude to hold given the fleeting nature of existence.

Rooted in Taoism and Zen Buddhism, wabi-sabi encourages a mindset that embraces reality **as it is**, devoid of the ego's craving for perfection. It asks us to stop fretfully imagining some other place, some other time when everything will finally be worked out and perfect. It asks us to courageously face the fact that this, right here, right now, is our life. Warts and all, it is what it is. When we accept and embrace life as the "wonky" thing it is, we teach ourselves acceptance and contentment with the present moment. We gently shift away from the mind's chatter and toward a state of mindfulness and peace. This is the genuine peace of acceptance—not the illusory peace of perfection.

With practice, we learn that there is a stillness and beauty in things that are flawed. We can feel love and fondness for our life in the same way we might love a chipped mug or a well-worn pair of old socks—these things are not perfect, but they have their own dignity and worth. Once we can practice accepting small imperfections in our world, we can expand that compassion and extend it to ourselves. Are our personal "flaws" really flaws at all, or are they the endearing little scratches and bumps that give our existence its character and uniqueness?

A way to apply wabi-sabi in your life is to do a "half-ass" challenge. This is a (lighthearted) way to crumble the ego-based attachment we have to getting things done perfectly.

Step 1: Identify a task

Select specific activities or tasks where intentionally doing things less than perfectly is feasible. Obviously, you don't want to be a heart surgeon experimenting with doing a so-so job on a patient, so use your discretion! To start practicing the art of imperfection, choose something small. This may involve daily chores like washing dishes, exercising, or organizing clutter.

A small warning here: watch out for the perfectionist tendency to do even this task as perfectly as possible. Deliberately choose something small and humble—you are not required to attempt a grand, overnight lifestyle transformation! As an example, let's say you identify an area where you have particularly high standards that are objectively unnecessary: your dishwashing routine. Doing things just right in this area is often a source of stress for you, and you have a whole host of beliefs around keeping your kitchen sink and surrounding area "perfect."

Step 2: Establish intentional limits for these tasks

For instance, leaving one item in the sink instead of washing all dishes, or leaving a few little sprinkles of water on the countertop so it looks a little less than perfectly tidy. Choose something that feels meaningfully imperfect to you. This may be walking on the treadmill for nineteen minutes forty-six seconds, rather than an even twenty minutes. It may mean cooking a recipe where you know you don't have all the ingredients and will have to improvise. It may mean giving yourself just five minutes to draft an email and sending it off after those five minutes, whether you think you've done it perfectly or not.

Setting these limits helps create a deliberate boundary against perfectionism, preventing it from becoming an excuse for procrastination. It's a little like training yourself to tolerate—and even enjoy—things that are imperfect, unfinished, impermanent.

Step 3: Listen to the inner voice pushing you to do more, speed up, or give up entirely on tasks

As you start experimenting with these little acts of playful rebellion against perfection, you will encounter resistance. Face this, too, with an attitude of acceptance. Your experience with learning to embrace imperfection will itself be imperfect! Try to hold it all in kindness and, if you can manage, a sense of humor.

You may notice that as you're working on a project at work, a voice tells you to keep editing endlessly or else to abandon it because it's not perfect. Just notice this voice and see what happens when you consciously choose not to engage with it. See it coming ... and see it going again. If you like, challenge it. Show your fear that settling for "good enough" actually won't result in any disasters.

Your sink, for example, can be in a constant state of untidiness as a flow of dirty and clean dishes passes through it day by day. Isn't this more interesting, more beautiful even, than a picture-perfect sink that is always clean? Maybe you notice that submitting a report that meets the basic requirements without obsessing over every detail can still lead to positive outcomes. In fact, it can bring a sense of relief and freedom knowing that you've completed the task adequately and can move on to other priorities. Occasionally, something special and unexpected emerges from the imperfection—a new perspective, opportunity, or solution arises where we did not think to look for it initially.

Wabi-sabi is ultimately not an exercise or a series of steps, but rather an attitude, a mindset, and a way of doing things. Nothing in life is consistent. Nothing is ever truly finished. And even things that are beautiful and seemingly perfect will eventually decay with time. There is so much stress and friction in trying to force life to be what it isn't. If we can accept life on its own terms—that is, as impermanent, changing, incomplete, flawed—then we are free from all the mental energy spent on either clinging to or avoiding certain expectations and demands.

A life filled with wabi-sabi is one that joyfully finds beauty in things that are culturally assumed to be ugly or worthless. It requires the courage to be a little unconventional, and to ask, are old things really less valuable than new ones? Has a chipped teacup lost something—or has it maybe gained something? Is your suffering, failure, and discomfort really a mistake? Is beauty something static and invulnerable, or is it a flow and a movement, something that is always changing?

Wabi-sabi frees, empowers, and relaxes a needlessly busy mind. Your thoughts are powerful. Perfectionist overthinking will turn your awareness into judgment, finding fault everywhere. But with a softer, gentler attitude, you can start to see the fullness in things right now, just as they are. Can you be happy *now*, even though things aren't exactly as you wish? Can you love something that is only partway lovable? Can you choose to be content in this moment and not wait for some moment in the future that actually hasn't happened yet?

A few more wabi-sabi-inspired tips:

- Don't be too hard on yourself . . . or others.
- If you notice yourself procrastinating, challenge yourself to start even if you're unsure or not feeling ready.
- Shift your focus from outcomes to process. Instead of seeing the marathon, just become curious about the next step forward.
- If you're feeling unhappy, scared, lonely, angry, etc., can you find a way to see the value in that? After all, what happens to unhappiness when you are happy to have it?

- Be mindful about your media consumption and cut down on "inspirational" content that creates a panicky sense of needing to always do more.
- Learn to laugh at yourself. Who says you have to take any of it seriously?
- Think in terms of mental minimalism, and get rid of overthinking the same way you'd get rid of junk and clutter in your home. Instead of continually focusing on what's missing and what you don't have, ask yourself, what can you do without?

Learning to Tolerate Uncertainty

Wabi-sabi can help us embrace imperfection, incompletion, and impermanence. Another less-than-ideal facet of life is its uncertainty—i.e., the fact that few things are guaranteed, and we seldom work with one hundred percent conviction about outcomes. We don't always possess complete information, and we cannot always predict how events will turn out. Life, in other words, is always unfolding and never under our complete control.

You may have noticed that your overthinking is an attempt to regain a degree of **control**. In the face of not really knowing something for sure, we may resort to endless "research" and overanalysis, churning ideas around in our head in the hopes of coming to a conclusion that will finally relieve us of the unbearable ambiguity of it all. Imagine, for example, someone waiting for the results of an important medical test. Do they have the dreaded disease or don't they? It's an unknown. The uncertainty is excruciating. As they await the test results, they start to feel that they would even settle for a bad outcome if it only meant they'd know that outcome for certain!

Research has consistently shown that uncertainty significantly increases discomfort, even when there's no objective difference in the perceived threat's intensity. People exhibit greater stress when faced with a fifty percent chance of a shock compared to a one hundred percent certainty of one. Studies in this area consistently show that people would choose certainty even if it came with significant penalties. We seem to have an innate aversion to uncertainty and will seek to reduce it even if it costs us dearly. In a way, it does cost us dearly—if we are accomplished overthinkers, we may already know that our anxiety about an unresolved situation is very often worse than the situation itself!

But what's so bad about uncertainty?

Look closely and you will see the effort to reduce uncertainty everywhere in everyday life, like repeatedly contacting loved ones, impatiently Googling symptoms while we wait for a doctor's appointment, or compulsively refreshing inboxes, all so we don't have to endure *not knowing* for any longer than we have to.

Our intolerance of anxiety has neurological and evolutionary roots, and our efforts to avoid it have been found to correlate with heightened activity in areas like the amygdala and anterior insula. Uncertainty tolerance is closely connected to anxiety, hypervigilance, and the way we appraise and react to risk.

Dealing with uncertainty is a fundamental aspect of daily life, as the future is inherently unknown. While individuals certainly differ in their ability to tolerate uncertainty, the fact is that life is fundamentally uncertain. This means that the onus is on all of us to learn to better understand, tolerate, and even thrive on uncertainty, rather than ignore it or get caught in the trap of trying to "fix" what is essentially not ours to fix.

Anxious people, particularly those who worry excessively, tend to have a low tolerance for uncertainty and often resort to overplanning, overpreparing, and overthinking to avoid it.

While it's normal for people to feel some discomfort with uncertainty, being highly intolerant of it can lead to constant efforts to control situations and can hinder adaptability to changing circumstances. Here are a few signs that your own uncertainty tolerance is not yet well-developed:

- You constantly seek reassurance or validation from others.
- You may not know what you think or feel until you know other people's opinions.
- You're a slave to your to-do list and use it as a tool to impose structure and control over even small details of daily life.
- You sometimes get caught in "research mode"—but it only seems to make you feel less sure of things.
- You feel like you lack confidence and don't believe you have the ability to cope.
- You are impatient and sometimes try to prematurely "force a conclusion" instead of waiting.
- You have difficulty trusting others to lead, especially if you don't fully understand a situation or process. You'd prefer to be the one in control.

A way to tolerate uncertainty is to act AS IF

Just because uncertainty crops up in your life, it doesn't mean you have to react and immediately do something to counter it. Uncertainty won't kill you—even if it sometimes feels like it will! If you're a low uncertainty-tolerance person, that's okay. You can teach yourself to be more comfortable and at ease with life's innate open-endedness. Try the following steps:

Step 1: First, make a list of thoughts and behaviors that you engage in to alleviate uncertainty or avoid it altogether. It may take a little while to start recognizing these thoughts and behaviors for what they are. This could include seeking reassurance, double-checking, or procrastinating. Without judgment, start keeping track of these thoughts and behaviors day to day, and notice how they're functioning in your life.

Step 2: Rank the behaviors and thoughts according to the level of anxiety you would feel if you couldn't engage in that behavior. Rate on a scale from one to ten, with one being only mild anxiety, and ten being extreme anxiety. This will allow you to put these behaviors in order. For example:

Behaviors that alleviate or avoid uncertainty	Anxiety level
Doing other people's work for them because you can't be certain they'll do it right	10
Phoning/messaging/checking up on people when they're out because you're not certain if they're okay or when they're coming back	10
"Following up" on someone else's task before necessary because you don't like not knowing what's going on	8
Checking and rechecking your phone to find evidence that the new person you're dating likes you, because it's uncomfortable not knowing how they feel	6

You can have as many items on your list as you like, but you will probably notice a few recurring themes—for example, you may see that your uncertainty intolerance is more pronounced at work, and your attempts to avoid it take on predictable forms, such as second-guessing others and micromanaging their work.

Step 3: Now practice building your uncertainty tolerance by selecting small behaviors from your list to try to resist doing. Start with the least anxiety-provoking ones and work your way up. Pick a behavior and commit to avoiding it a few times in a week, observing how it feels and what happens when you refuse to engage. For example, you might deliberately assign a task to a colleague. You feel stressed not knowing for certain whether they'll do it or do it correctly, but you notice this feeling and choose *not* to engage with it. You don't email or call them to check. You don't allow yourself to dwell on the idea.

Step 4: Write it all down. Keep a record of each instance where you act as if you're tolerant of uncertainty (i.e., you act in a way opposite to what your ordinary impulse suggests). Document the following:

> *What exactly did you do or not do?*
>
> *How did you feel while doing/not doing it?*
>
> *Was it harder or easier than you thought?*
>
> *How did everything turn out?*
>
> *Did things turn out okay even though you were not one hundred percent certain?*

> *If things did not turn out as planned, what happened? How did you cope?*
>
> *What have you learned about yourself and your ability to respond to life?*

Sometimes the only way we can convince ourselves that the world won't end just because we endured a little uncertainty is to actually make ourselves endure a little uncertainty. Keep track of your progress and how your assumptions and predictions may change over time, as you gather more counterevidence for the idea that uncertainty is unbearable. You may discover that it is slightly uncomfortable or a little unpleasant at times . . . but it's not quite the disaster you thought it was.

Amor Fati and Being a "Yes-Sayer"

An unexpectedly helpful concept in the quest for cultivating uncertainty tolerance is *amor fati*, translated as "love of fate" in Latin. This is a philosophical concept that encourages us to embrace and love our "fate" regardless of its nature. Central to this idea is the acceptance of life's uncertainties and the pursuit of meaning even in challenging experiences. The concept is traced to Epictetus and Aurelias, but gained more prominence with existential thinker Nietzsche, who wrote on the idea of the eternal recurrence—i.e., the happy willingness to live exactly the same life again and again, forever.

Nietzsche wrote:

> "My formula for greatness in a human being is *amor fati*: that one wants nothing to be different, not forward, not backward, not in all eternity. Not merely bear what is necessary, still less conceal it—all idealism is mendacity in the face of what is necessary—but love it."

Elsewhere saying,

> "I want to learn more and more to see as beautiful what is necessary in things; then I shall be one of those who makes things beautiful. *Amor fati*: let that be my love henceforth! I do not want to wage war against what is ugly. I do not want to accuse; I do not even want to accuse those who accuse. Looking away shall be my only negation. And all in all and on the whole: someday I wish to be only a yes-sayer."

Amor fati is a strange concept that nevertheless has a lot to teach us about releasing our desire for control and certainty. Instead, it encourages seeing every aspect of life, including suffering and loss, as either beneficial or necessary. This is a more expansive, practical take on acceptance—we embrace what is because, on a fundamental level, it is our "fate." Though this word may have lost some of its meaning today, it is not about fatalism or being apathetic or despondent. Rather, it's about having a positive and accepting attitude toward the unfolding of one's life journey—including that portion that is as yet shadowy and unknown to us.

Applying *amor fati* in your life involves:

- Acknowledging and embracing **everything** that happens in your life, without judgment or resistance. This includes both positive and negative experiences. Understand that resistance to the present moment often leads to anxiety and discontent. In fact, it is often the *only* source of this anxiety and discomfort. Instead, practice living in the present moment and accepting what is happening right now. Take physical pain as an example: Accept its existence rather than denying or wishing it away. Acknowledge that it has already happened and take constructive steps to address it.
- Instead of viewing negative experiences as inherently bad or

harmful, see them as opportunities for growth and self-improvement. Practice reframing setbacks, failures, or disappointments as necessary parts of your journey. Embrace adversity as a chance to practice virtue and resilience. Cultivate gratitude for the lessons and growth opportunities that arise from challenging circumstances, rather than dwelling on the pain or suffering itself.
- Recognize that some things are simply beyond your control and learn to embrace uncertainty rather than resisting or fighting against it. Practice letting go of attachments to outcomes and accepting that everything in life is temporary and constantly changing. Embrace impermanence as a natural part of the human experience.
- Develop self-compassion by treating yourself with kindness and understanding, particularly during difficult times. Recognize that suffering and failure are inevitable aspects of life, and offer yourself words of encouragement and acceptance.

Improv Thinking

Uncertainty means we cannot predict how things will unfold. But there is no rule to say that this is inherently a stressful or vulnerable state to be in. After all, we often find great joy and pleasure in things precisely because we cannot know the outcome—puzzles, riddles, stories, surprises, games, and even the game of flirting and falling love. None of these things would be half as valuable if we knew the outcome ahead of time.

Another area where unpredictably is fun rather than threatening is in improv comedy. A joke is, by definition, something we don't know the punchline to, right? In the same way, improv shows us that staying in the uncertain present and playfully allowing the future to unfold in an unpredictable way is a brilliant method for cultivating acceptance, good humor, and deeper trust in the flow of things. There is some evidence to suggest that participating in improv increases divergent thinking, tolerance of uncertainty, and overall well-being (not to mention it's a lot of fun!).

The concept of uncertainty tolerance involves the psychological responses, both negative and positive, triggered by the awareness of ignorance about certain aspects of the world. Uncertainty stems from three sources: **probability, ambiguity, and complexity**. Probability relates to the randomness of future outcomes, ambiguity concerns the reliability of information, and complexity involves features that hinder our understanding.

Improv encourages participants to embrace uncertainty without judgment, fostering a mindset that welcomes unpredictability—and plays with it. This shift in perspective enables people to navigate uncertainty more effectively and adapt to unexpected challenges with creativity and resilience.

How to Develop an Improv Mindset (Without Signing Up for an Improv Class . . .)

Practice ambiguity: Embrace uncertainty by acknowledging it rather than avoiding or denying it. Get comfortable with phrases like "I'm not sure" or "Who knows?" The point is to sit with the feeling of uncertainty rather than rush in to resolve it. Realize that you can have no opinion, and you can be undecided. You can be in process. You may not know the answer now, but you might know it later.

Accept what is: In improv, you are never creating a scene on your own. You co-create, which means that things are always partly out of your control. This is not a problem! The old improv mantra is "play the scene you're in." That means accepting what's actually going on onstage instead of forcing some kind of agenda about how you think things *should* go.

In real life, this means clearly parsing out what's in your control and what's not. It also means being realistic about the facts of a situation and not wasting time and energy arguing with those facts. Rather than longing for a different past or speculating about an unknown future, focus on making the most of the present moment. Ask yourself questions like "How can I make the most of this?" and "What are some ways I can make this work?"

Work with what you got: The "yes, and" rule in improv emphasizes building on what is real and what is actually happening right now. The idea is to never resist or deny a prompt from another improv member to take the scene in a different direction. Rather than saying, "No, but," to a new development, you say, "Yes, and."

Okay, so things are evolving in a way you didn't quite anticipate. Say yes to that. Then, add what you like. Pick up that thread and run with it rather than wasting time trying to go back to some past moment that is already gone, or forcing the situation in a direction it can't/won't go. Is there a way to get what you both want? Things may be taking a path you didn't anticipate, but can you update your goal? Can you get creative, think on your feet, and adapt as you go?

How to Cultivate Helpful Thinking

By learning to embrace imperfection, tolerate uncertainty, and go with the flow of the unknown, we can find, paradoxically, a kind of stillness in the chaos of life. From this position of stillness, another paradox is that we begin to really appreciate our mind and what it can do for us. If you have an allergy, you are suffering because your immune response to certain neutral stimuli is overactive. But when you treat the allergy and your immune system calms down, it settles into its more natural function in your body and can then carry on with the business of serving you (i.e., protecting you from genuine threats) rather than getting in your way.

The mind is the same. When it is overactive, undisciplined, unfocused, or inflamed, you suffer. But in treating this overactivity and learning to find stillness, control, and acceptance, you are better able to appreciate the natural and normal function of your mind—and that function is to help you be happy! Your mind is there to help you solve problems, create, analyze information, make sense of the world, predict and prepare, set goals, learn and grow, plan a response to setbacks, and stay focused and organized, to name just a few.

When you suffer from anxiety, it makes sense that all you want to do is get rid of your mind, which can start to seem like a kind of torture device. The mind is certainly a terrible master, but remember that it is also a wonderful servant. The solution to overthinking is not less thinking, but better thinking. It is not automatic, unhealthy, and self-sabotaging thinking, but thinking that is conscious, healthy, and helpful.

Developing an optimal, helpful thinking style is in fact the goal of all cognitive behavioral therapies, and the goal of much of what has been covered in this book already. The ongoing premise has been this: your thoughts, feelings, and actions are all connected. The way that you think about a situation influences how you feel, as well as what you choose to do. The situation does not cause our emotions and force our responses; instead, the way we think, interpret, and give meaning to the situation is what influences our thoughts and actions.

Therefore, if we want to change the way we feel and behave, where should we put our efforts? The cognitive behavioral model says we should pay attention to our thoughts. Are we engaging in helpful thinking? Or unhelpful thinking? Are the thoughts we entertain helping us feel what we want to feel and behave as we want to behave? Are our thoughts going to enable us to live the life we want to live? This is the essence of making your mind your servant.

One caveat before we continue, however. Cognitive behavioral therapy (CBT) techniques should only be attempted when you are feeling calm and composed, and not in the middle of an active worry or panic spiral . . . at least not initially. You'll already know that trying to rationally argue against your overthinking mind just doesn't work in the heat of the moment. What's worse, desperately trying to fight and control your "negative" thoughts can backfire, as you end up engaging with those worries more than you should. The techniques we'll discuss are best done in preparation for those tricky moments when worry and rumination start to take over, and not once you're already on the back foot, so to speak.

So, what is helpful thinking? We can define it as a perspective or a style of thinking that consciously considers all aspects of a situation and forms conclusions based on facts about the self, the world, and others. It's balanced, realistic, and practical. It's what thinking looks like when it's given a job to do, and that job is the creation and fulfilment of a meaningful life, however you define that. You may be very familiar with *unhelpful* thinking, but it takes a little practice to learn to recognize and cultivate thinking that is "on your side." One way to do that is to keep a helpful thinking diary.

Helpful Thinking Diary

Putting your thoughts down on paper can help declutter your mind, allowing for clearer thinking and the feeling of calm and contentment that grows from that. In the diary, you will write down all the things that your anxious, overthinking mind is predicting, as well as your level of belief in those predictions, and how that belief impacts your emotions.

By carefully putting things down this way, you can start to appraise them more neutrally and realistically. You can look for real evidence for and against the predictions you're making and assumptions you're holding. You can work through the worst case, best case, and most likely case, as we covered previously, and explore the consequences of attaching to each of these potential outcomes.

Finally, you can use your diary to explore possible alternatives, ask questions, re-evaluate, and possibly make adjustments to your original predictions. How does slowing down to think more helpfully change how you feel? How you act? You gather all this data, and in time and with practice, helpful thinking becomes more natural to you.

Here are some steps to start keeping a diary, but bear in mind that the only characteristic of a helpful thinking diary is that it's *helpful*! That means that you can and should experiment with the format so that you personally are getting the most from the process. Your goal is not to correctly follow a sequence of steps or produce a nice-looking worksheet, but rather to develop your ability to take a step back from your own thinking process and start to make it work for you.

Broadly, the steps are:

1. **Write down your worries.** What are you stressed about? Put it in words and put labels on how you feel. Be neutral and nonjudgmental.

2. **Start to question these thoughts and interpretations**. Ask yourself:

- What are you predicting is going to happen? Usually, you are predicting that something bad is going to happen, so be specific and write down *exactly* what it is you fear might happen.

- How strongly do you believe this will happen? Rate the strength of your belief between zero and one hundred percent.
- What emotion(s) are you feeling? Without judgment or interpretation, put as fine a label on this as you can.
- How intense are these emotions? Rate the intensity of your emotion(s) between zero and one hundred percent.

3. **Try out some helpful thinking.** Here are some useful questions to ask yourself to get the "helpful thinking juices flowing":

   - What is the evidence for my prediction?
   - What is the evidence against my prediction?
   - What is the worst that could happen? And what could I do to cope?
   - What is the best thing that could happen?
   - What is the most likely thing that will happen?
   - What are the consequences of worrying about this?

- What is a more helpful way to view the situation? What advice would I give to a friend feeling this way?

4. Based on your answers to the questions in your diary, you will then come to a more **helpful conclusion** by asking:
    - What would be a more balanced and helpful thought to replace my worry?

5. The final step is to **re-rate**:
    - Re-rate how much you now believe the original prediction you were making.
    - Re-rate the intensity of the emotions compared to what you were originally feeling

If you consistently apply this strategy, you're likely to notice a reduction in your belief in negative predictions and a decrease in the intensity of your emotions. Noticing this alone will be an interesting experience—what an insight, to realize that you have always been at liberty to make these changes and adjustments! You realize that the big reward is not to feel some "positive" emotion, but rather to master your own self-regulation and gain greater awareness and acceptance of the emotions you do feel, and a deeper appreciation for how these thought patterns are playing out in your life. Keep practicing. It may require time, persistence, and practice, but gaining the ability to perceive life in a more balanced way will be highly rewarding in the long run.

However, if you *don't* find this process helpful, that's okay too. Remember that you are developing the capacity to think helpfully—you are not attempting to reach a particular outcome. If the process isn't working, become curious about why that is. Ask how you feel before and after you start making notes in your diary. Change things up and notice what effect this has. Ask yourself, if this isn't working, then what will? Remember, *you* are in control. What does that look like?

The Goal: Make All Your Thinking Helpful Thinking

Emotionally balanced, healthy people tend to have helpful thinking as their default mode. This is not a superpower but simply something they are good at because they've had enough practice to make it habitual. Every time you consciously choose to adopt a helpful rather than harmful thinking mode, you are strengthening this ability in yourself.

Over time, the diary will not be necessary anymore because you will be able to run through the process quickly and automatically without prompting. Even when you encounter an exceptionally difficult or confusing situation, you will know to pause, take a step back, and look carefully at what you're thinking. You know that you don't always have to look at the world from inside your thoughts, but can look at the thoughts themselves. A few more helpful questions:

- Am I in a "thinking trap" or a cognitive distortion (such as all-or-nothing thinking or catastrophizing?)
- Have I confused a fact with a feeling? For example, just because I *feel* attacked, does it mean I actually am being attacked?
- What would I tell a friend or loved one who was engaging with this thought?
- What assumptions and foregone conclusions am I making?
- Have I gotten confused between "possible" and "certain"?
- Is this thing I'm worried about a disaster/horror/calamity, or is it just an inconvenience/unpleasantness?
- Have I had this worry in the past? What ultimately happened? How did I cope?
- What resources do I currently possess that could help me cope with the worst-case scenario?

- What is fact and what is pure guesswork about the facts? Am I "filling in the blanks"? Is it possible that I simply don't know much about this thing I'm worried about?

Try to remember that learning to think helpfully is not about penalizing or denigrating your anxious or "negative" thoughts. You are never trying to catch yourself out or shame yourself into thinking more "rationally." After all, if you merely replace your anxious overthinking with self-critical overthinking about how anxious you are, you haven't made much progress!

There is a great kindness and compassion in just being neutral. Step away and gently refuse not to make any judgments at all about things. Remember that you always have the option not to react. When we are anxious and overthinking, we tend to assume that:

Our thoughts are the same as reality.

Our thoughts are true.

Our thoughts are important.

Our thoughts are orders or directives that we cannot ignore.

Our thoughts are wise.

Our thoughts are who we are.

When we think more helpfully, we learn to recognize that the thoughts that pop into our minds are *not necessarily* true, important, wise, or irresistible. They may be . . . but then again, they also may not be. Perhaps they are only partly true or only somewhat important. When you detangle from your thoughts this way, you start to realize that your thoughts, and what you choose to do with them, are all optional.

Thoughts are tools. One way of living is to notice that you only have a toolbox full of hammers and to assume that you can do nothing about it but go around in life hitting nails, whether you like it or not. Your tools determine what you can do—i.e., the thoughts you have are in control, and they determine your actions and your feelings. When someone says, "I'm a loser. I can't start my own business," it is much the same as saying, "I only have hammers in this toolbox. All I can do is hit nails; I can't do anything else!"

But you can also take a step back and realize that *you are in charge of the kind of tools you have in that toolbox*. You can look at the world and decide on your own goals, and then stock your toolbox with things that will help you achieve those goals. If you want to build a house, for example, then you can carefully and neutrally kit yourself out with all the things you'll need to make that dream a reality. Your tools are there to help you build the life you want—i.e., your goals and values determine what thoughts you choose to have. Asking yourself if your thoughts are helpful or not is just like asking, "Is this toolbox really letting me do the things in life that I want to do? What can I get rid of and what do I need to have that I don't currently have?"

A great exercise is to imagine the kind of person you want to be, living the kind of life you want to live, and doing and feeling the kind of things you want to do and feel. Now, ask yourself, what kind of thoughts does this person have? In other words, how do you have to think in order to be the kind of person you want to be? That is the essence of helpful thinking.

Summary:

- Non-anxious people do not have easier or calmer lives. Rather, they have a different way of responding to the same obstacles, stresses, annoyances, and unknowns we all face. One thing they embrace is imperfectionism, or wabi-sabi—the courage to be calm and well amid a life that is forever incomplete, imperfect, and uncertain.

Perfectionism is about holding impossibly high standards and is closely connected to overthinking, anxiety, and procrastination. The solution is recognizing your tendencies and choosing to challenge them with compassion, rather than more rules, demands, and expectations.

- Wabi-sabi embodies simplicity, humility, gracefully accepting imperfection, and seeing the beauty in aging and the passage of time. By embracing life for what it is, we gain the genuine peace of acceptance, not the illusory peace of perfection. A way to apply wabi-sabi in your life is to do a "half-ass" challenge: Choose a task and establish intentional limits to its accomplishment. Listen to the voice of perfection when it arises, and let it go with compassion.
- Anxious overthinkers tend to have a low uncertainty tolerance and often try to escape or avoid it, but we will never have complete control in life or absolute certainty about outcomes. Carefully identify behaviors you engage with in order to reduce uncertainty, and experiment with not doing these behaviors, observing the

results—"as if" you are uncertainty tolerant, and in time, you will be.
- The philosophy of *amor fati* and elements from improv thinking can help you embrace uncertainty and enjoy your "fate," whatever that may be.
- Helpful thinking is not automatic, unhealthy, and self-sabotaging, but thinking that is conscious, healthy, and effective at helping you achieve your goals, in line with your values. It's balanced, realistic, and practical.
- A helpful thinking diary can help you consciously consider all aspects of a situation and form conclusions based on facts.

Chapter 6: Move Forward

Stress and overthinking can be "managed." With effort, patience, and compassion, anxiety can be treated and gradually unlearned. The ultimate goal, however, is to live a life where we are not constantly defining ourselves in terms of what we are worried about. At some point, we can abandon anxious thought patterns entirely and start to get curious about how we want to grow, create, and change—i.e., how we want to move forward in life.

Anxiety can be incredibly distressing. But arguably the worst thing about it is all the things it prevents you from having—such as spontaneity, joy, confidence, exuberance, bravery, and authenticity, to name a few. In our final chapter, we are looking at ways to move on from anxiety, specifically better ways to make decisions, take inspired action, and solve life's problems in ways that will bring you real change and growth.

Overchoice: How to Avoid Analysis Paralysis

Michelle doesn't really consider herself an overthinker or an anxious person, with one important exception: She *hates* having to make decisions. If she has to go shopping for something, choose a tradesman to do work in her home, or pick a TV series to watch, she quickly finds herself drawn into a spiral of stress that doesn't have an end. She tries as hard as she can to make the best decision, but the more she attempts to whittle down the options and carefully weigh everything up, the more flustered and overwhelmed she gets. Eventually, she becomes so annoyed that she just picks something—anything—as long as it means no longer having to keep analyzing the options.

Michelle's anxiety around this "overchoice" means she has avoided making big house moves or going on complicated travel adventures, and she often finds herself deferring to other people so that they just make the choice for her—with mixed results. Sometimes the anxiety isn't even relieved by making a decision, anyway, and she finds that her worries just shift focus: "Did I choose the right thing? What would have happened if I had chosen the other thing?"

Analysis paralysis happens whenever people are presented with an overwhelming number of choices or possibilities, leading to difficulty in making decisions. In Michelle's case, this represents a very particular kind of overthinking and rumination, one that is triggered and exacerbated by an overabundance of information in the environment. For some of us, uncertainty is an anxiety trigger, and for others, anxiety crops up most after a stressful event. For Michelle and other sufferers of analysis paralysis, the trigger is an array of options that are simply too great to properly process.

Plenty of choice may seem like a good thing, but the paradox of choice refers to the phenomenon where having an abundance of options can actually lead to feelings of paralysis, stress, and dissatisfaction rather than freedom and satisfaction. The more options, the more there is to think about, and the greater the chance that you'll miss out on the "best" one. Barry Schwartz, an expert on this phenomenon, describes how the presence of too many choices can overwhelm people's cognitive processes, causing them to get stuck in decision-making, finally leading to a sense of regret or dissatisfaction with the chosen option.

Making a decision or choice between options is always a little stressful. Facing a fork in the road, we are aware that our choices can and will have real consequences for our lives, whether it's just selecting breakfast cereal or choosing a career or life partner. Knowing this, we are also aware of the threat of loss and the real possibility of making a choice that brings us to a worse place than where we are now.

Logically, the mind then goes into analysis mode. It tries to process all these options and their likely outcomes. If it can identify only the best option, then it can choose that option as soon as possible and so relieve the mounting sense of stress that comes with being undecided. Right? Though this reasoning makes a kind of mathematical sense, the truth is that real life seldom poses easy answers to the question "Which is best?" The only answer we can find is often "It depends."

Option A may make sense from a financial point of view, but not a social or emotional one. Two options may look equal but play out on different time scales—what then? One option may look really promising, but is that just because you are very aware of the pros and relatively unaware of the cons? How are you going to define *best*, anyway? And what if you make a decision that takes you on the wrong path, and you can't change your mind?

Prolonged contemplation of this kind feels like problem-solving behavior but is actually far from it—it can intensify feelings of threat, uncertainty, and discomfort as you become increasingly fixated on finding the "perfect" solution. This makes you less rational and effective, not more. Yes, perfectionism and analysis paralysis are closely related!

The fear of making the wrong decision can also trigger a cycle of rumination where you envision various scenarios, imagining worst-case outcomes and dwelling on the potential risks associated with each option. If ruminating over the worst-case for a single situation is stressful, imagine how much more stressful it is to ruminate over several possible situations—or even infinite ones!

When it comes to approaching options, there are two kinds of people: Maximizers are individuals who tirelessly strive to make the best decisions by exhaustively exploring all available options, often feeling the pressure to achieve perfection and fearing missed opportunities. In contrast, satisficers aim to find options that meet their criteria or standards, choosing the first satisfactory option without engaging in exhaustive comparison.

While maximizers prioritize optimization and may experience higher stress levels, satisficers prioritize satisfaction and tend to be more content with their choices. When Michelle, a maximizer, goes to the supermarket and tries to buy peanut butter, her overthinking turns on and she starts trying to identify the absolute best peanut butter to buy. She'll think about the price, the taste, the ingredients, the brand's ethics (Does it contain palm oil? Is "sustainable palm oil" better or worse than having no palm oil at all?), the nutrition profile, the value for money, whether it's locally made, chunky or smooth, has a nice jar design, and so on and so on and so on . . .

Someone else may walk into the supermarket, recognize a peanut butter brand they bought a few weeks ago, recall that they liked it, and buy another jar. Then, they forget all about peanut butter and move on with their lives (if it wasn't obvious, this is a satisficer). Did they get the best possible jar of peanut butter? Well, maybe not. But they got a pretty good jar, and they only had to spend twenty seconds choosing it.

Maximizers can fall into the trap of noticing that they are getting stressed and overwhelmed, and wrongly assuming that the way out of that anxiety is to *analyze more*. Instead, if you're like Michelle, try to take a page from the satisficers' book. Make your new goal to find a path that is good enough, rather than one that is the best.

To stop yourself from falling into analysis paralysis, try to cultivate a satisficer's mindset. This may be challenging if you're a perfectionist, and may often go against social and cultural norms. But it does get easier:

1. **Ask yourself what your goal is.** Sounds obvious, but many people burn themselves out trying to optimize on a choice that doesn't even really matter to them either way. In other words, the reason you can't decide on what to choose from the menu is simply because you're not hungry! Whether it's purchasing a coffee maker or picking a mobile phone network, remind yourself of your objective. What is this particular choice helping you to achieve in life? Analysis paralysis can often be worse when we are unclear on what we're trying to achieve.

2. **Establish criteria or standards that align with your goal.** Overthinkers tend to assume that it's desirable and possible to take into account *all* parameters—it's not! Only some factors in the decision-making process are relevant to you. Avoid unnecessary complexities and focus on what truly matters. For the coffee maker example, if you determined that your goal is to make excellent coffee at home, then prioritize factors such as quality when looking for a model. If your goal is more about getting something straightforward to occasionally make coffee for guests, then you may choose to focus on something that is small, simple, and affordable. Refrain from getting entangled in minute details that may not significantly impact your overall outcome.

3. **Accept "good enough" options.** Embrace the idea that perfection is not always necessary. In fact, it seldom is. Be honest and ask if a particular option is still capable of satisfying a need or goal without being one hundred percent perfect in every way. Instead of tirelessly pursuing the absolute best, recognize when an option meets your

defined criteria and is "good enough." Then move on. This approach reduces stress and frees you from overthinking. Whether it's a coffee maker or any other decision, choose what aligns with your preferences, and move forward without dwelling excessively on minor differences. Let's say you find a machine at a store that you like the look of; it ticks all the boxes and is the right price. Plus, it's right in front of you! You accept that you could theoretically keep optimizing in tinier and tinier ways (could you save five dollars by buying from somewhere else?), but this option is good enough, and so you choose it confidently, without second-guessing yourself.

Ask "The Watch" or Ask "The Squad"

FOMO is the fear of missing out, and the closely related FOBO is the fear of a better option. The more we allow these two forces to control us, the more likely our decision-making will become impulsive, reactive, and overly emotional.

The modern world is chaotic and information-soaked, with many vested interests seeking to actively stir up and exploit the human tendency to worry about missing out or making a mistake. Advertising, the news, and social media all play on our fears that others could be busy right now living a happier and more fulfilling life than we are.

The pressure to optimize is constant, but should we commit to making a concrete choice, we are instantly thrown into doubt about what we might have lost by choosing that thing instead of some other thing. We may find ourselves anxiously flitting from one choice to another, never quite settling, or else we are paralyzed and apathetic, not quite able to choose anything.

In his book *Fear of Missing Out: Practical Decision-Making in a World of Overwhelming Choice*, author Patrick McGinnis explores strategies to identify, pause, and manage both FOMO and FOBO. Each of his techniques begins with critically examining the information guiding our choices and understanding the stakes involved.

According to McGinnis, not all decisions are created equal, and it's worth learning to discern the difference. He believes decisions can be categorized into three levels:

High-Stakes Decisions

These are choices that can significantly alter our lives, such as major financial investments, career changes, or life-altering commitments like marriage. They require careful consideration due to their potential long-term effects.

Low-Stakes Decisions

These decisions have some importance but are less significant than high-stakes ones. They may include everyday choices like what to eat for dinner, what movie to watch, or which route to take to work. While they matter to some extent, their outcomes typically don't have a lasting impact.

No-Stakes Decisions

These decisions have minimal or no consequences. They're often fleeting and inconsequential in the grand scheme of things. Examples might include choosing between two similar options that won't have a lasting impact on your life or forgetting about the decision shortly after making it, such as which brand of dental floss to buy.

It's important to know which kind of decision you are trying to make, and not confusing a low-stakes decision for a high-stakes one. That said, less important decisions still have their place—mastering decisions deemed as low- or no-stakes is just as crucial as navigating high-stakes moments. This is because the majority of decisions we encounter daily fall into these categories. Despite their seemingly insignificant nature, these choices do gradually accumulate and influence the tone and quality of life. For overthinkers in particular, the way we engage with these constant low-stakes decisions can consume significant time and mental energy, creating enormous anxiety and decision paralysis.

Here's a way out:

Know What the Stakes Are

When a decision comes to your awareness, ask yourself:

Is the decision fleeting? In other words, will you have forgotten all about this decision in a week? A month?

Does this decision have few/no significant consequences in your life or the lives or others, whether that's money, time, or other impact?

Can you live with your choice no matter what the outcome is?

If you answer yes to all the above, chances are you're dealing with a no-stakes (you'll forget it in a week) or a low-stakes (you'll forget it in a month) decision.

For No-Stakes Decisions, Ask "The Watch"

Streamline decision-making by reducing options to two choices and using a random tool to make the final decision. Give yourself a time limit. This technique, discussed in the TED Talk "How to Make Faster Decisions," helps overcome trivial decision paralysis. With practice, it becomes a natural and efficient way to handle low-consequence choices, reclaiming time and reducing stress caused by FOMO and FOBO.

For Low-Stakes Decisions, Ask "The Squad"

Seek input from a trusted circle of individuals, your "squad," to make informed decisions swiftly and without emotional bias. Present them with a clear dilemma and ask for their opinion, using closed questions for straightforward choices and open questions for broader input. Avoid involving your squad in trivial, no-stakes decisions. Naturally, you have to make sure you trust your squad!

What about the high-stakes decisions? That's more complicated and will require all your analytical power. This means, however, that you don't want to waste any of that power on the low- and no-stakes decisions. Says McGinnis,

> "You have a limited amount of time and mental energy to spend on all the decisions you make each day. When you exhaust that energy before the day's choices are done, you don't have the strength to keep your hands on the wheel—and FOMO and FOBO are happy to take over."

If you waste time and energy analyzing what doesn't matter, you don't have any left for the decisions that do. If you catch yourself in analysis paralysis, try to remind yourself that almost *all* our day-to-day decisions are insignificant in the grand scheme. Take the pressure off. Spend effort identifying what matters and let the rest go.

Reversing the Anxiety Spiral

Adam is an overthinker. He's also socially anxious and self-conscious, which means he finds socializing scary and stressful. The same pattern always unfolds for Adam: Someone will invite him to a social event, and knowing that he should make efforts to be friendly, he accepts. But in the lead-up to the event, Adam's rumination grows steadily more intense as he worries about how it will turn out.

As the day approaches, he's so anxious he almost feels sick. His rumination starts to make up elaborate stories about why he doesn't want to go, he can't go, and in fact he *shouldn't* go to the event. His self-talk starts to concoct elaborate justifications and excuses for why it's foolish to go—the event is not that important, it doesn't matter if he goes, the person inviting him didn't really mean it anyway, and besides, he may be coming down with a cold, and it may be smarter to listen to his "intuition" and stay home for some well-deserved self-care . . . and on and on.

So, he cancels. The moment he does, he feels a flood of relief. His anxiety melts away, and he no longer feels sick. That proves it, he thinks. It must have been a bad idea to go after all. So, Adam stays home that evening. Had he pushed himself to go out, he might have had a range of interesting and unexpected experiences. He might have met some people he liked, had a good time, and discovered that once he warms up, he can indeed manage and even enjoy social situations.

But Adam experiences none of this when he stays home. The next time he's invited out, he has only a few experiences to draw on: the fact that socializing seems to make him feel awful, and the fact that not socializing feels a whole lot better. He makes a "rational" decision and declines the invitation again.

Adam tells himself that he is shy, easily overwhelmed, and an introvert. He sincerely believes that turning down almost all social invitations is his way of *managing* anxiety. The truth is actually the other way around: His habit of avoiding social events is itself causing and worsening his anxiety.

In cognitive behavioral therapy, practitioners will often talk about "reversing the spiral" of anxiety, panic, and rumination. Let's take a closer look at this spiral and the role that overthinking and rumination may play.

Step 1: You anxiously scan your environment for signs of threat or danger.

Step 2: Because you're scanning in this way, you are both creating more physical sensations (for example, an increased heart rate) but also sharpening your attention so much that any neutral sensation becomes interpreted as a threat and seems larger than it is ("Am I having a heart attack?!"). Your attention narrows, and all your focus goes further inward, to yourself and your inner experiences.

Step 3: To deal with this threat, you may decide to avoid or escape the situation somehow.

Step 4: For a moment, escape "works" because you feel relief. This confirms it for you—the thing you perceived really was dangerous after all. You teach yourself that avoidance and escape is necessary. However, this relief is only temporary.

Step 5: By teaching yourself that the stimulus really is dangerous, and that you really are unable to cope with it, you actually increase your anxiety and worry in the long term, lose confidence in yourself, and find that the thing you're avoiding seems scarier than ever.

Step 1: You land back at the beginning of the spiral, except this time, when you scan your environment for threat and danger, you seem to find even more threat than you did before . . .

To summarize, anxiety can lead to avoidance, which (only temporarily) reduces anxiety, and this brief relief reinforces your avoidant behavior. You "stay safe," but in the process you reinforce your faulty beliefs and assumptions (i.e., that there is something to stay safe from in the first place) and teach yourself to be even more anxious in the future.

In Adam's case, his avoidance means that he never exposes himself to any situation that might provide counterevidence for some of his core beliefs. His avoidance *feels* like a solution in the short term, but it isn't really in the long term. In the same way, temporary discomfort and unfamiliarity doing something new may *feel* a little uncomfortable in the short term, but in the long term it is incredibly beneficial.

Avoidance reinforces the cycle. So, what can we do to break it? Well, the opposite of avoidance is **approach**.

Repetitive, intrusive, and negative thoughts keep you trapped. Overthinking is often one way we can indulge in avoidance—it's the mental story that accompanies our avoidant behavior (i.e., we *think* so that we don't have to *do*).

These stories may feel comforting in the moment, but they only keep us standing still, going in tighter and tighter circles. While we waste all our precious brain power on things that are insignificant, we are simultaneously missing out on the opportunity to genuinely learn to face and overcome our fears. By staying at home, the only lesson Adam learns is to be a more and more accomplished avoider; he never learns to tolerate and cope with social stress, he never acknowledges or improves on the strength and abilities he already has, and he never gets to prove to himself that mild social discomfort is not, in fact, the end of the world.

Imagine a spiral or cycle; all its energy and motion keeps it moving in the same place. There is a lot of movement, but paradoxically, it doesn't go anywhere. It never covers any new ground. But if you can remove the spiral's center of gravity, it suddenly spins out and can move. It can now travel linearly, and you get a straight line. In this analogy, healthy thinking is powerful, purposeful, and directed. It takes you from A to B.

Fear is an opportunity to practice helpful thinking and to use your mind's power to help you *move forward* instead of getting trapped in the ineffective anxiety spirals.

Graded Exposure

One way to approach what you're anxious about and move forward is a technique called graded exposure. The idea is to gradually confront, rather than avoid, feared situations. Slowly, you build your confidence and start to gently challenge any unhelpful assumptions, beliefs, and expectations about yourself and the world. It's not a punishment, however! You start with small, manageable challenges and work your way up, bearing in mind that the point is to condition a new response:

    1. Identify your feared situation.

2. Break down the gap between where you are now and where you need to be into small, manageable steps, constructing a "ladder" that increases in how much anxiety it provokes.

3. Start with the first rung of the ladder and expose yourself to the situation.

4. IMPORTANT: stay in the situation until you feel calmer. If you escape at the height of your anxiety, you only reinforce the avoidant behavior. Instead, "stay with" the fear until it subsides.

5. Only when you are fairly comfortable with one rung on the ladder, move on to the next, continuing until you have faced your greatest fears without needing to escape or avoid.

Let's see how Adam could use graded exposure to help tackle his social anxieties. He first constructs his graded hierarchy (i.e., the ladder), and it looks like this:

- Go for a coffee with a close friend.
- Go for a coffee with two close friends.
- Go for a coffee with a close friend and a stranger.
- Go for a coffee with a stranger.

- Attend a meetup with more than three people.
- Attend a meetup with more than ten people.
- Attend a small meetup where you don't know anyone.
- Attend a big meetup where you don't know anyone.
- Attend a big meetup where you don't know anyone, and take the initiative to talk to three new people.

The way you construct your own hierarchy will be completely unique to you and your situation. Spend some time on this, ensuring that the jumps between each "rung" are roughly equal and not too big. Choose things that are realistic but still meaningfully challenging for you, and make sure the order is correct.

Adam starts with the first task, meeting a close friend for coffee. But simply exposing himself is not enough; he needs to notice his anxiety and consciously stay in the situation until it subsides—i.e., teaching himself a new response that counters his tendency to avoid or escape.

In practice, your anxiety probably won't disappear, but it should reduce. What's important is that you don't escape. Repeat each rung of the ladder as many times as you need to. Do not move on if you are feeling absolutely terrified. While avoidance and escape are not on the table, that doesn't mean you can't make adjustments and tweaks as you go. If you need to break the next rung down into two smaller rungs, that's okay. Similarly, if you're feeling confident, feel free to do a little more than you planned. Remember, you are in charge!

This process may take some time, but then again, think about how many years of your life you have spent mastering your avoidant and "safety seeking" behaviors, and be patient with yourself. You never have to force anything. You might like to incorporate breathing or relaxation exercises into each exposure attempt to help bring your anxiety level down. Some people find it helpful to keep a diary where they can monitor their anxiety levels (rate on a scale of one to ten) and keep track of their goals and progress.

As you go, keep noticing the effect the exposure is having on certain assumptions, beliefs, and expectations. For example, Adam may have the core belief that he is somehow different from everyone else (probably a little worse?) and that everyone thinks he's weird and can tell when he's anxious. Bit by bit, though, he notices his belief in these ideas lessening. He starts to gather evidence for the idea that most people are barely paying attention to him at all, let alone judging him. As he works through his graded exposures, he simultaneously works to challenge and reappraise his cognitive distortions. He keeps checking in on the facts. Did his predictions come true? Did the worst happen?

Transform Overthinking into Problem-Solving

In way, overthinkers are blessed with an unexpected superpower. Overthinking, when channeled in the wrong way, can wreck your life. But what about if it's channeled in the *right* way?

The secular, Western mindfulness movement that's popular today tends to paint all mental activity with the same brush: if it's not full, unattached conscious awareness in the moment, then it isn't mindful. But this view doesn't acknowledge that there is a difference between a controlled and an uncontrolled mind. The "monkey mind" of Buddhist lore is not *all* mind—it's only mind that is reactive, undisciplined, unfocused.

The mind, as we've said over and over, is a tool. It's possibly the greatest tool that has ever existed. It has immense power, range, variability, resilience. An out-of-control mind can be quietened . . . but it can also be **harnessed** and put to use solving problems, creating, or optimizing.

Overthinkers are often encouraged to take up meditation and mindfulness, and these practices can be enormously helpful. But there is nothing especially sacrosanct about the present—rather, the value comes in mastering one's own consciousness so that it can be willfully brought to the present *when desired*, and willfully taken to the past or future when that is necessary, as it is when planning, learning from mistakes, and so on.

A flexible mind under your conscious control is one that can relax and let go of stress at night when it's time to sleep, but also wake up and summon all its resources to focus on a tricky work problem the next day. It can loosen up and explore when it wants to be creative, or it can knuckle down and work methodically through a detailed task. None of these states of mind are better or worse; rather, what matters is your ability to switch between them. Your well-being and effectiveness are not about maintaining perfect Zen-like enlightenment at all times. What matters is your ability to maintain purpose, intention, and focus as you move through all different states of mind.

Overthinking is the mind doing what it's meant to, but in an uncoordinated and ineffective way. Overthinking is distorted problem-solving. So, what does effective problem-solving look like?

One dictionary definition of "think" is "to direct one's mind toward someone or something; to use one's mind actively to form connected ideas." That's the first big difference between thinking and rumination: The former is constructive, connected, and purposeful. The latter is not. When we use our brain power to solve problems (rather than create more for ourselves!), we identify real issues, generate solutions, weigh up those possibilities, and choose the best path forward. Then we put a plan in place to take rational action. Afterward, we assess the results, adjust, and take further action.

Rumination and overthinking, however, tends to focus only on things that haven't happened yet, or else things that have already happened and can't be changed. It fundamentally can't come up with any new solutions or alternatives, because it is only focused on things that we have no control over. The big difference between real problem-solving, and the illusory problem-solving of overthinking, is **conscious action**.

A few questions to ask before you embark on a more practical mode of problem-solving:

- Is there even a problem at all?
- If there really is, is it *your* problem?
- Is the problem you see actually happening right now, or is it something you're just guessing/predicting will happen?
- Does this problem genuinely require your immediate action?

If you have a genuine problem that is currently unfolding, it is your responsibility and requires your immediate response, and then you can move on to the next consideration: Is the problem solvable? Examples of solvable worries include financial obligations, work tasks, and interpersonal conflicts, whereas unsolvable worries revolve around unpredictable future events or circumstances beyond one's control. By distinguishing between solvable and unsolvable worries based on their realism, likelihood, timeliness, and controllability, you can better identify which concerns warrant problem-solving efforts ... and which may simply require your tolerance and acceptance.

Six Steps to Solving Problems

Let's imagine that you've started to ruminate over the gas and phone bills, and you find yourself worrying about whether there's enough money. You quickly run through the above questions and determine that this is an appropriate problem to work on. Instead of overthinking, you commit to using your brainpower to solve the very real problem at hand:

Step 1: Identify/define the problem

Clearly state the problem, focusing on observable behaviors and circumstances. In this case, the problem is that the gas and phone bills are due at the same time, and there isn't enough money to cover both. Clearly acknowledging the problem may be difficult in itself, since there could be some avoidance. For example, you don't look at your bank balance or open bills that arrive in the mail for fear of what you'll see. In this way, rumination, avoidance, and fear of the unknown all work to increase anxiety.

The first step is to be completely honest. Realistically appraise the facts and just the facts. Define the issue in neutral terms in the way a disinterested third party might.

Step 2: Generate possible solutions/options

Your anxious mind may want to start dwelling on catastrophic outcomes ("What if they cut the gas off? How will I live without a phone? What if I descend into abject poverty and have to live under a bridge by next month?"), but ignore all this. Keep your focus on all possible solutions here and now. At first, when brainstorming, you'll be prioritizing quantity over quality. Without prematurely assuming anything, just put down as many ideas as you can.

In our example, some options include negotiating payment plans with the companies, prioritizing one bill over the other, putting the bills on a credit card, borrowing money, or seeking assistance from a financial counselor. You may also put down more "out there" options, which include robbing a bank, running away from home, and selling your granny's rare Ming vase on eBay (chances are you won't do any of these, but write them down anyway).

Step 3: Evaluate alternatives

Only once you've brainstormed as much as you can, assess the advantages and disadvantages of your solutions. Rank them on factors like effectiveness, feasibility, and potential consequences. For example, negotiating payment plans may allow for keeping both services but could be embarrassing, while prioritizing bills may result in temporary inconvenience. Whittle down your options to a few most promising possibilities and draw up a pros and cons list for each. If you tend toward analysis paralysis, take care that you are focusing on one specific goal only—in this case, it's preserving both utilities with limited funds. Your temporary discomfort and embarrassment levels also matter, but they may not warrant endless analysis since they don't connect to your main goal.

Step 4: Decide on a plan

Choose one or more solutions to implement, specifying who will take action, when, and how. Often, we may feel like we have no options, but it's more accurate to say that we don't really *like* the options we have. That's okay! But remember that you always do have options. For instance, contacting the gas and phone companies to negotiate payment plans could be scheduled for Monday morning, followed by seeking assistance from a financial counselor in the afternoon. You may decide that calling on a friend can serve as a last resort.

Clearly identify:

- What actions you will take

- When you will take them
- What you will do given the outcome of that action

This way, you are piecing together an action plan that keeps you focused. Don't rely too heavily on just a single option since it may not work.

Step 5: Implement the plan

Put the chosen plan into action as outlined, following through with the specified steps and timelines. Again, this may not be pleasant or comfortable, but taking action in this way is usually far more tolerable than mindless worry and rumination!

Step 6: Evaluate the outcome

Reflect on the effectiveness of the plan, considering whether the problem was adequately addressed and if any adjustments are needed. If necessary, revisit the problem-solving process to select a new option or revise the existing plan based on the outcome.

You might have noticed something: Nowhere in the six steps is anxiety necessary. This is an important point. Feeling stressed, nervous, or terrified is actually not required for us to effectively solve our problems. How liberating to know that we can always choose the very best strategy to move forward and improve our lives, and not a single moment of anxiety is needed.

Summary:

- Analysis paralysis happens whenever people are presented with an overwhelming number of choices or possibilities (overchoice), leading to difficulty in making decisions. To avoid this, aim to be a satisficer, not a maximizer. This means accepting "good enough." Identify your goal, set standards, and stop when you find an option that meets these standards.
- FOMO is the fear of missing out, and the closely related FOBO is the fear of a better option. To overcome them, first understand whether a decision is high, low, or no stakes. For a no-stakes decision, "ask the watch"—i.e., whittle choices down to two and then quickly make the decision. For low-stakes decisions, "ask the squad"—i.e., a trusted group of friends or mentors who will be able to give you an unbiased view. Save most of your mental energy for more complex high-stakes decisions.

- We can learn to reverse the anxiety spiral by turning avoidance and escape behaviors into *approach* behaviors, using the technique of graded exposure. Create a graded hierarchy of anxiety-inducing situations, but prevent yourself from escaping/avoiding until you condition a calmer response. Then move on to the next rung of the ladder. Anxiety can lead to avoidance, which (only temporarily) reduces anxiety, and this brief relief reinforces your avoidant behavior and cements faulty beliefs and assumptions. Avoidance strengthens the cycle; approach breaks it.
- Overthinking conceals a superpower; when mental energy is harnessed and channelled, it can be put to use solving problems, creating, or optimizing. A flexible mind under your conscious control is one that can move between states deliberately, according to your goals and values. In healthy problem-solving, we identify the problem, generate possible solutions, weigh them up, take inspired action, and assess the results—no anxiety required!

www.ingramcontent.com/pod-product-compliance
Lightning Source LLC
Chambersburg PA
CBHW061747070526
44585CB00025B/2816